D1573085

Cartooning Texas

Cartooning Texas

*One Hundred Years
of Cartoon Art in the Lone Star State*

Maury Forman
and Robert A. Calvert

TEXAS A&M UNIVERSITY PRESS
College Station

Copyright © 1993 by Maury Forman
Manufactured in the United States of America
All rights reserved
First edition

The paper used in this book meets the minimum requirements of the American
National Standard for Permanence of Paper for Printed Library Materials, Z39.48-
1984. Binding materials have been chosen for durability. ∞™

LIBRARY OF CONGRESS CATALOGING-IN-PUBLICATION DATA

Cartooning Texas : one hundred years of cartoon art in the Lone Star State / [edited
　　by] Maury Forman and Robert A. Calvert.
　　　　　　　　p.　　cm.
　　　　ISBN 0-89096-560-9
　　　　　1. Texas—Politics and government—1865–1950—Caricatures and
　　cartoons. 2. Texas—Politics and government—1951– —Caricatures and car-
　　toons. 3. American wit and humor, Pictorial—Texas.
　　I. Forman, Maury B., 1950–　.　II. Calvert, Robert A.
　　F391.C35　1993
　　976.4'06'0207—dc20　　　　　　　　　　　　　　　　　　　93-1570
　　　　　　　　　　　　　　　　　　　　　　　　　　　　　　　CIP

To Mary Foye,
whose love and understanding
have been with me
throughout Cartooning Texas.

—M. F.

Contents

Acknowledgments

This book was made possible due to the kindness, generosity, and talent of many people. First and foremost are the cartoonists who have done or continue to "do time" in Texas and whose works appear in this book and are now a part of Texas history. I am especially grateful to Ben Sargent, Etta Hulme, and Jimmy Margulies, who have encouraged me from the start and allowed me to interrupt them even when they were on deadline. I am also grateful to David Horsey, Brian Basset, and Chris Britt, whose work inspires me on a daily basis.

I would also like to thank the families of Texas' early cartoonists, who welcomed me into their attics and storerooms and loaned me original cartoons for use in the book and the touring exhibit. This includes Mary Ficklen, Eloise McClanahan, Ann Taylor, Phillip Martin, Jo Ann Cole, and Jack Patton, Jr.

Cartooning Texas would have been a much more difficult project if it were not for the excellent preservation skills of the archivists of Texas' best libraries. These include Marsha Anderson, Thelma Stone, and Kim Nicholson of the Fort Worth Public Library, Joan Dobson, Jimm Foster, Paula Barber, and Carol Roark of the Dallas Public Library, Roger Rainwater and Nancy Bruce of the Mary Coutts Burnett Library at Texas Christian University, Doris Glasser and Doug Weiskopf of the Houston Public Library, Steve Stappenbeck, Ralph Elder, and Trudie Croes of the Barker Texas History Center, University of Texas, Austin, and Mary Ellen Holt and Michael Hazel of the Dallas Historical Society.

I am especially indebted to Richard West, Richard Marschall, and Lucy Caswell, who are the best cartoon historians in the country; Mike Price, Milt Priggee, and Bruce McDonald for doing an incredible job in cleaning up the text and cartoons; Georgia McWeeney and Kathy Rann of Banana Printing and Graphics for making the cartoons visually correct; and Sara Clark, Bob Darden, Mary Elizabeth Jackson, Brad McMillan, and especially Eric Blumberg for providing some important and necessary research.

I also would like to acknowledge Jack Tinsley of the *Fort Worth Star-Telegram*, Margaret Walker of the *Houston Post*, Tony Pederson of the *Houston Chronicle*, and Bill Evans of the *Dallas Morning News* for allowing permission to reprint the editorial cartoons first seen in their papers and for allowing editorial cartoonists to practice their craft on a daily basis. Special gratitude goes to Mark J. Cohen for the loan of several of the cartoonists' caricatures in the back of the book. On a more personal side there were people who believed in this project and provided financial and nonfinancial support at just the right times. These include Ellen Katzen, Rich and Kim Dickman, Karen Kenter, Virginia Foye, and Brian Foye, who provided food, lodging, and transportation during research trips; Bill Archer, Joan Wright, and Chase Untermeyer for steering me in the right direction; Billy Goldberg and Frances "Sissy" Farenthold, who first got me interested in politics; Elton Lipnick and Elizabeth Gunter, who believed in me as much as in the project; Michael Kahn, who provided the necessary financial and technical support to bring this project to a successful conclusion; and Joshua and Adam Forman, whose love of learning and cartoons inspired this book.

Finally, a special thanks to Gayla Harris and Mike and Diana Campbell, whose friendship I once lost but then found and whose presence in Texas encouraged me to continue this book.

—M. F.

Introduction

For a political cartoon to be successful it must create an intellectual and emotional response in the reader. For that reason, it is impossible for a political cartoon to be well received unless it is about a topic that is extremely important to a widespread cross-section of the reading public. The key to the success of the cartoonists chronicled in this book is their ability to address the critical issues of the day incisively and concisely.

This book then is essentially Texas history in the raw. It is a compilation of the visual commentaries of brilliant (and not so brilliant) journalists about the issues and people most on the minds of Texans for the last one hundred years. Whether this book is a cartoon history of Texas, or a Texas history of cartooning is irrelevant. One of the most remarkable aspects of this one hundred–year period is the continuity of the subject matters and cartoonists that have dominated the interests of Texans and therefore their political cartoons.

The cartoons and politics of every decade chronicled in this book are centered around hotly contested, controversial, and colorful political campaigns—usually for the governor's chair. In this book you will meet (or reacquaint yourself with) a fascinating array of flamboyant politicians, ranging from the controversial Governor Hogg, to the incomparable Ma and Pa Ferguson, to the inexorable Governor Shivers and the remarkable Pappy O'Daniel. Texas also contributed numerous unforgettable politicians to the national scene, including Vice-President John Nance Garner, Vice-President and President Lyndon Baines Johnson, longtime Speaker of the House Sam Rayburn, Treasury Secretary John Connally, Vice-President and President George Bush, citizen Ross Perot and others whose faces and exploits were cartoonists' fodder over the years. In short, the cartoons that follow present dozens of mini-biographies of Texas-sized leaders who engaged in political and ideological crusade after crusade over the last one hundred years.

The issues that have dominated Texas life have remained remarkably constant over these one hundred years. First and foremost, Texas has been deeply touched by economic issues. Not surprisingly, therefore, in every decade you will see (that is the beauty of a cartoon—you actually *see* the subject matter) the agitation of Texans over taxes, government spending, government corruption, the prices of goods and services (and labor). Moreover, again not surprisingly, the prices of cotton and oil as well as the solvency and efficiency of large railroads and financial institutions are of constant interest over time. Even browsing through these cartoons, you will be struck at the applicability of many old cartoons to the concerns of today.

Another strain of continuity concerns the theme of people's rights. The cartoonists have consistently chronicled civil rights (African-American, Hispanic, and immigrant), workers' rights (including the consequences of strikes, voting rights) and woman's rights issues. Additional issues relating to public schools, including financing, curriculum, and sports, have been in the public's mind and eye through this period. These issues—like economic and political ones—have remained constant themes of public concern from decade to decade.

In sum, this kaleidoscopic history of Texas provides wonderful proof of the teaching that there is nothing new under the sun. Perhaps it also will allow us to read today's political cartoons with the wisdom that we have survived and prospered despite the fact that we have already experienced all the political, economic, and social crises we again face today.

CARTOONING TEXAS

The Decade of Beginnings (1890–99)

The 1890s were years of remarkable ferment in politics, the economy, and even in journalism. The decade was not always the Gay Nineties, especially to those caught in a cruel depression, to those suffering crises in the farm economy, or to restive revolutionaries in political movements like Populism.

Texas was at the southern end of the belt in America that was the focal point of all this political ferment—Mary Ellen Lease in Kansas urged farmers to "raise less corn and more hell!"—and Texas cartoonists reflected, reported, and reacted. Notable cartoons during the decade naturally documented the local and statewide political wrangling, but they also serve today as mirrors of the larger issues at play. Cartoonists like William Sydney Porter and Elmer Burruss were prescient enough to recognize the issues—such as industrial trusts and railroad regulation—underlying the specific, transient squabbles. In their work they foreshadowed concerns that would last a generation in American politics.

Likewise, the 1890s were a period of ferment in journalism, nationally and in Texas. The proliferation of photoengraving, allowing even local papers to be freed from invariable columns of gray type, or primitive-looking chalk-plate drawings, enabled newspapers and their cartoonists to promptly comment on issues. The increasing number of newspapers in Texas during this decade of growth provided a Petriedish for the nascent field of graphic satire. And, finally, there was the phenomenon of Texas' own journalistic industry: the humorous journal.

Texas Siftings was a magazine of national circulation actually edited in New York City. Its focus was more humorous than political, but it provided raw material for building Texas' reputation. The *Texas Sandwich*, on the other hand, had more bite. A satirical journal edited in Dallas and aimed at a statewide, rather than national, audience, it took on a variety of topics and personalities. Issues of this weekly newspaper, once thought lost to history, were recently found in an old cheese box through the luck and persistence of a Dallas librarian. The paper was published between 1893 and 1902.

The most interesting of the Texas comic papers was the *Rolling Stone*, published in Austin between 1894 and 1895. It carried clever satire on society and politics of the time in text and cartoon, but it also is notable because its editor and chief cartoonist was William Sydney Porter— later known to the world by his nom de plume, O. Henry. Porter, a bank teller, bought the weekly *Iconoclast* from publisher W. C. Brann. He changed the title, filled the paper with bright but excruciatingly rendered chalk-plate cartoons, and attracted national attention. Unfortunately, this publicity was not matched by support from Texas advertisers, and the *Rolling Stone* gathered no more moss after about a year of publication. Ironically, the paper reverted to publisher Brann, who renamed it the *Iconoclast*.

Porter moved to Houston, where he wrote and drew for the *Post* with much success and to great acclaim. However, his career was interrupted by an indictment for embezzlement from the Austin bank where he had worked while publishing the *Rolling Stone*. He quit his job on the *Post* and took a banana boat to Honduras. Wanting to be closer to his family, he returned to Austin to face the charges and was sentenced to five years in prison. While in prison, he perfected his literary craft and never drew another cartoon. He gradually began to sell stories, but not wanting to use his real name, settled on O. Henry.

The drawing styles of Texas cartoonists of the 1890s is what observers might today, in hindsight, charitably call naive and enthusiastic. There is a crudeness that in most cases does not mar the sincerity or a very real conceptual force. But if the sophistication of the art work looks uneven to us, even when we compare cartoons with the same signatures, it is probably because these enthusiastic craftsmen relied on references: the flavor (and in some cases actual figures or compositions) is of prominent New York cartoonists like Joseph Keppler, F. Opper, and Dalrymple. But little matter—the Texas cartoonists did well their jobs of fashioning their resources to fit statewide themes and issues.

A POLITICAL COON HUNT.—Texas Cartoon.

"A Political Coon Hunt"
H. M. Peace
June 12, 1890
Southern Mercury

A grass-roots farm organization, the Texas Farmers' Alliance, swept across the state in the 1890s, enlisting more than two hundred thousand men and women in its ranks. Many members endorsed the candidacy of James Hogg for governor in 1890. Hogg, as a reform attorney general (1887–91), had warred with special-interest groups, which he thought were bilking Texans. In particular he had fought railroad monopolies, endorsing what emerged as the Texas Railroad Commission to regulate the carriers. His opponents tried to defeat his nomination as the Democratic candidate for governor in 1890 by uniting conservative forces against a railroad commission. This cartoon in the *Southern Mercury*, at this time a strong Hogg journal, portrays the attorney general and his supporters treeing the anti-commission forces, which tried to deny him the 1890 nomination.

A VERY LITTLE GIANT
ON A VERY RICKETY PLATFORM.

GOULD TOUCHES THE BUTTON, GEORGIE TRIES HARD TO DO THE REST.

"A Very Little Giant . . . "
Cartoonist unknown
October 22, 1892
Texas Farmer

James Hogg won the nomination for the gubernatorial election in 1890. The legislature passed a commission law in 1891; as Hogg wanted, the members of the commission were appointed rather than elected. Conservative Democrats bolted the party and nominated George Clark, who opposed the commission. This cartoon shows Clark as an unworthy opponent standing on a weak platform composed of disgruntled Democrats. One side of the platform is held together by Republican support, an allusion to the endorsement of Clark by the important African American Norris Wright Cuney. The notorious Jay Gould, a railroad magnate, who was deemed in folklore and by many historians as corrupt, is the force that holds the "rickety" platform upright.

WHAT WE MAY EXPECT WITH WOMENS' SUFFRAGE.

"What We May Expect with Woman's Suffrage"
Elmer Burruss
June 17, 1894
Texas Sandwich

Women unsuccessfully petitioned the constitutional conventions in 1868 and 1875 for the right to vote. In 1893 women organized the Texas Equal Rights Association. That organization undoubtedly prompted this 1894 cartoon. In this rather standard attack on woman's suffrage, the artist depicts women as using the issue of voting as a Trojan horse to seize control of the man's accepted role in society and to force males to become caretakers of the home. Also note the implication that all women who advocated voting rights were unattractive and their male supporters were effeminate. The issue became more volatile after the turn of the century. Women achieved the right to vote in Texas and national elections with the ratification of the Nineteenth Amendment to U.S. Constitution in 1919. Texas was the first southern state and the ninth state overall to ratify the Nineteenth Amendment.

"By Gatlins, I'll See that Uncle Sam Don't Send Any Troops to Texas."

"Hogg"
William Sydney Porter
July 29, 1894
Rolling Stone

Not all newspapers, of course, endorsed Governor Hogg and his policies. The *Rolling Stone*, a weekly devoted to tongue-in-cheek humor and satire, enjoyed making fun of the governor, his policies, and his mannerisms. It is not clear if editor William Sydney Porter was anti-Hogg for his policies or simply saw the governor as an easy target at which to poke fun. Porter draws Hogg as a frontier ruffian, armed to his teeth, determined to defend Texas against any federal troops. The canteen hanging from Hogg's belt is labeled "Blood," a sly innuendo that Hogg was similar in philosophy to Gov. David H. "Bloody Bridle" Waites of Colorado, who had allegedly advocated violence in response to labor struggles in that state.

THE FATE OF SLANDERERS.

"The Fate of Slanderers"
Cartoonist unknown
August 4, 1894
Texas Farmer

Governor Hogg became involved in a national controversy in 1892 over the decision of Democratic president Grover Cleveland to send federal troops to Illinois to break the Pullman strike. They were sent despite the objections of Illinois governor John Peter Altgeld. Hogg sided with Altgeld, holding that Cleveland's actions violated states' rights and the Constitution of the United States. George Bailey, a reporter, wrote up an account of the speech Hogg delivered in New York in defense of Altgeld's stand. The *Dallas News* ran a series of editorials condemning Hogg and accusing him of calling for state sovereignty at the expense of order and of endorsing labor radicalism. Hogg responded to the criticism in a public address at San Antonio. Hogg is depicted here as stomping his enemies with his San Antonio explanation of his actions.

"And now, young man (turning to General Culberson), when you take the mansion, I trust your path may not be studded with briar patches like mine has been."—Gov. Hogg's Speech at Capitol.

"And Now Young Man . . . "
William Sydney Porter
September 1, 1894
Rolling Stone

Charles M. Culberson had been attorney general in the Hogg administrations. E. M. House, a political organizer of great ability who had managed Hogg's earlier campaigns, supported Culberson for governor in 1894 and secured for him first place on the ticket. Culberson won again in 1896. He went to the U.S. Senate in 1898 and served there for the next twenty years. Hogg retired from political office, and this cartoon was drawn from the former governor's last speech, where he wished the newly elected Culberson success. Among the "briar patches" that Hogg supposedly wrestled with was the depression of the nineties, entitled "no credit" and "empty treasury," labor violence, as depicted by the bomb, numerous railroad antitrust suits, and intemperate speeches (at least according to the cartoonist) at San Antonio and elsewhere.

The Planks that Held the Pops Went Down.

"The Planks That Held . . . "
Elmer Burruss
November 25, 1894
Texas Sandwich

The 1890s witnessed the organization of the Populist party, or the People's party. Texas Populists nominated Thomas L. Nugent for governor in 1894, but he lost to the Democratic nominee, Charles A. Culberson, by a vote of 216,373 to 156,000. Here, scattered by the Culberson whirlwind, are seen Populist candidate Nugent and two leaders of the party, H. S. P. "Stump" Ashby and James H. "Cyclone" Davis. The strewn "planks" of the platform represented how opponents characterized the Populist goals. Note the woman's suffrage issue in the right-hand corner of the platform and the allegation of Populist sympathies for black people, with the racial epithet on the left side of the image.

Tribulations of Texas Railroad Owners.

"Tribulations of Texas Railroad Owners"
William Sydney Porter
December 14, 1894
Rolling Stone

The Texas Railroad Commission was created in 1891 and given extensive powers during the governorship of James S. Hogg. Most important, it could set railroad rates and enforce them. Governor Hogg made John H. Reagan the first chairman of the commission. During 1891, the commission established rates on many products, including cotton and lumber. The railroads responded in April, 1892, by claiming in federal court that the commission's actions were unconstitutional and thereby getting an injunction against its rates. For two years, while the case was in litigation, the courts tied the hands of the commission. The Supreme Court ruled on May 23, 1894, in *Reagan* v. *Farmers Loan and Trust Co.* that the commission's powers were constitutional, and the commissioners went back to setting rates.

This cartoon by O. Henry depicts the state agency and the attorney general robbing railroads by enforcing rate regulations and suing for overcharges.

The Texas Santa Claus dislikes
 To slight a single stocking,
But then the number hanging up
 Is absolutely shocking.

Of candidates there are three score
 And each expects a present,
So when the gifts will not go round
 It's awfully unpleasant.

So, boys, when Christmas morning comes,
 If you are disappointed
Don't cry a bit nor let your faith
 In Charley be disjointed.

For filling ninety stockings up
 With only thirty apples,
Is certainly the hardest task
 That Santa Claus e'er grapples.

"Texas Santa Claus"
Elmer Burruss
December 23, 1894
Texas Sandwich

At the turn of the century, as now, one's political supporters expected political rewards for their election efforts. In this image, Charles Culberson is seen as Santa Claus, who must now give Christmas presents to those who exhibited good behavior in the November election. The spoils of office, as the poem says, were not numerous enough to go around. Various voting groups and organizers have hung their stockings on the mantel expecting political favors. Disappointed political bosses peer from behind the curtain. The implication on the part of the *Texas Sandwich* is that the governor has maneuvered his way into political office by promises to special-interest groups that he cannot keep. Note how cartoonists sometimes entered the literary world, combining their poetic talents with their artistic skills.

The Texas Hercules Tackles the Trust Monster,

"Hercules"
Elmer Burruss
January 27, 1895
Texas Sandwich

This pro-Culberson cartoon identifies him as the slayer of the evil trusts. Part of that image came from his activities as attorney general. Even though the new governor was more conservative than his predecessor, he did enforce antitrust legislation, including instituting a suit against Waters-Pierce Oil Company, a subsidiary of Standard Oil. Possibly the best description of Culberson's administration is that it blended together Hogg's reforms with the new governor's intent to go slowly in passing new measures.

Let Texas be Developed.

Texas has idle resources and the North has idle capital. If our lawmakers will keep unreasonable laws out of the way, the Goddess of the Lone Star State will yoke the two together and furnish employment for both.

"Let Texas Be Developed"
Elmer Burruss
February 23, 1895
Texas Sandwich

One of the ongoing dreams of Texas and the other southern states was to discover some way to attract northern investment capital into their region. Usually Texas legislators and business leaders pitched their pleas for capital investment by promising low labor costs, a favorable climate, cheap land, low taxes, and not much control over the way natural resources were exploited.

The political artist promises in this cartoon that if the legislature does not pass restrictive legislation (laws that would regulate corporate conduct), northern capital will move to the South and create employment opportunities. Despite many attempts to lure northern and foreign investments, Texas remained a rural state with little manufacturing development, except in raw materials, until World War II.

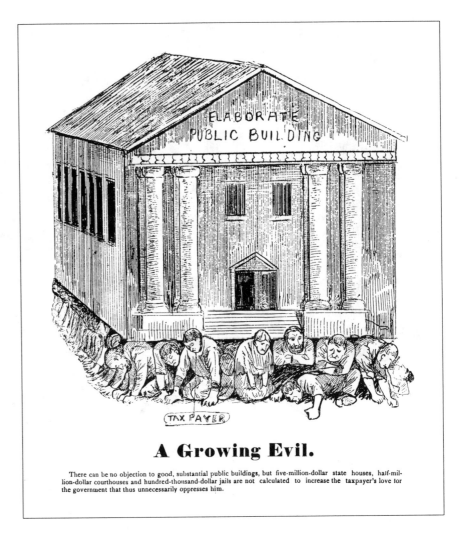

A Growing Evil.

There can be no objection to good, substantial public buildings, but five-million-dollar state houses, half-million-dollar courthouses and hundred-thousand-dollar jails are not calculated to increase the taxpayer's love for the government that thus unnecessarily oppresses him.

"A Growing Evil"
Cartoonist unknown
March 2, 1895
Texas Sandwich

In the tough times of the mid-1890s, taxpayer revolts erupted in agricultural communities all over the state. Many of these protests concerned the cost of state and county governments. This drawing shows public building expenses as an unwanted, unneeded, and elaborate government cost that oppresses taxpayers. The $5 million statehouse figure refers to the argument over the building of the state capitol authorized in 1879 and completed in 1888. In addition, the 1880s and 1890s saw the construction of courthouses as new counties were organized in the west. Although these expenses do not seem extravagant by present standards, embattled farmers saw the construction of public buildings as a celebration of politics and elected officials, or the elites, at the expense of the common person, or the taxpayer.

The Governor and the Lazy Legislative Boys.

THE GOVERNOR—"Boys, I told you to cut up this wood, but instead of doing it you have spent the time playing marbles and riding around on that flying jenny! Come up here, sirs, I will teach you a lesson or two, you young sleepy heads"—and he taught them.

"The Governor and the Lazy Legislative Boys"
Elmer Burruss
March 9, 1895
Texas Sandwich

Governor Culberson saw his role as one of demanding that the legislature provide economy in government. His tenure in office corresponded to the Panic of 1893 and hard times that lasted through 1897. The governor was determined to hold down costs of government through rigid administrative and judicial reforms. He believed one way to gain control of the legislative agenda was through liberal use of the veto. In this favorable depiction of Culberson's relations with the legislature, he is shown teaching the legislators a lesson about extravagance. Among the logs to be cut are free passes on trains, high fees for government and legal services, and, on the fence in the back, free excursions for legislators.

Going to market with 16 to 1 silver

What he bought with it.

Sixteen to One.

Those men who want free silver
Had surely ought to know,
That the better is their money,
The farther it will go.

And if they had their wishes
It would take a whole cart load
To buy enough provisions
To feed a common toad.

"Sixteen to One"
Elmer Burruss
June 22, 1895
Texas Sandwich

Beginning in the mid-1880s, some farmers demanded that silver be coined as legal tender at a ratio of sixteen to one—that is, that each silver dollar contain sixteen grains of silver for each grain of gold in a gold dollar. Farmers saw free or low-valued silver as an inflationary device that would allow them to pay off long-term debts with inflated crop prices. The Farmers' Alliance endorsed free silver in 1886, and eventually so did most southern Democrats, including Hogg and somewhat reluctantly Culberson, as well as all of the Populists. In 1896 the Democratic presidential candidate, William Jennings Bryan, ran as a supporter of free silver.

This political observer warns free silverites that if they win their demand, inflation will erode away purchasing power. The character pushing the wheelbarrow is drawn to resemble a rural villager: a warning to the middle class to stay with "sound" money, or gold coins, and avoid inflation.

16 TO 1 ON THE LONG HORN.

"16 to 1 on the Long Horn"
O. J. May
October 6, 1896
Houston Daily Post

In the 1896 gubernatorial campaign, the Populist candidate, Jerome C. Kearby, mounted a serious threat to the Democratic incumbent, Charles A. Culberson. As part of their campaign strategy, Texas Populists sought fusion with the state's Republicans, many of whom were African Americans. This was an especially interesting alliance in that on the national level Populists had fused with the Democrats in support of William Jennings Bryan's presidential campaign. The *Post*'s cartoon bet that Populist-Republican fusion would not succeed in gaining black votes for Kearby, using as odds the ratio made famous that year by Democrats and Populists who wanted "Free Silver"—the unlimited coinage of silver and gold at the ratio of 16 to 1. Kearby did not win, but he polled the largest vote ever by a Texas Populist statewide (44 percent) and carried eight of the sixteen counties with black majorities in the state.

TEXAS' ANSWER TO AN UNPARALLELED CAMPAIGN OF VITUPERATION, MISREPRESENTATION AND ABUSE.

"Texas' Answer"
O. J. May
November 6, 1896
Houston Daily Post

Gov. Charles A. Culberson, the Democratic incumbent, won re-election in 1896 over Jerome C. Kearby, the Populist challenger, who had been backed by the Republicans. The *Post* stands proudly by the victor while other major newspapers in the state slink away with the losers—Kearby, Barnett Gibbs (former Democratic lieutenant governor turned Populist), and E. H. R. Green (chairman of the Republican State Executive Committee). The campaign had indeed been vicious, but needless to say, Culberson's campaigners had given at least as much abuse as they had received. The laurels of victory amounted to a sixty thousand–vote majority rather than the seventy-three thousand votes the cartoon indicates.

"Sayers's Drawing Card"
Cartoonist unknown
October 20, 1898
Southern Mercury

In 1898 Joseph D. Sayers, a member of Congress, secured E. M. House's support for governor. Sayers had served briefly as lieutenant governor (1878–79) and had been congressman from 1895 until his nomination for governor. He triumphed in 1898 and won another term in 1900. The *Southern Mercury*, now a Populist paper, charged in October, 1898, that Sayers wished to buy political support and encourage fraud by investing the money in the Texas School Fund in bonds of other states and territories. That issue failed to create much enthusiasm for Barnett Gibbs, the Populist gubernatorial candidate, who lost the election to Sayers in November by more than 150,000 votes. Populist congressional candidates also ran badly. Sayers's easy victory notified Texans of the end of the Populist era.

Texas Cartooning
Comes into Its Own (1900–1909)

The growth of Texas came in bursts at the turn of the century, and not merely in terms of immigration and industrialization, sweeping as those phenomena were. Greeting the new century were such outpourings of mixed fortune as the Galveston flood and the wildcat oil boom around Beaumont. The flood claimed lives by the thousands—a disaster remembered in American folk poetry as the "Mighty Day of the Millennium"—but it also provoked a major engineering feat, the building of the Sea Wall, and the progressive reinvention of the City of Galveston. The Beaumont gusher foretold prosperity, but it also brought on a tide of opportunistic economic corruption, flooding an underdeveloped region with newcomers who scarcely had community interests at heart.

Rising to such occasions—some in spurts of immediate response, others in lasting artistry—came the cartooning journalists. As a class, they spent the 1900s defining the grammar of the editorial 'toon as we know it today, intensifying the ferocity of ridicule in general while specifically insinuating the trademark mascots (W. K. Patrick's duck, Tobe Bateman's goat) that would prove to be the ancestors of any number of signature characters.

Tougher grist for the cartoon mill was the wrangling between remnants of the old politics and forces of the new Progressivism, to say nothing of such colorful personalities as the former governor James Hogg and his abiding influence, Judge A. W. Terrell and his election reforms, and the disgrace-bound U.S. Senator Joseph Bailey. Texas occupied a vanguard point in the reform movement, leading other states in such areas as campaign guidelines, railroad-rate legislation, woman's suffrage, and child-labor laws. The Prohibition question became urgent, with controversies swirling about the efficacy of local option. And the Populist party was dissolving back into Republican and Democrat camps.

Point men among the Texan cartoonists were John Knott of the *Dallas News*, and Bert Blessington of the *Houston Daily Post*. The *News* was the paper that anointed cartoonists, with a history of running editorial drawings longer than any other Texas paper. However, other cities' dailies were right behind them. Prominent among the ranks of cartoonists were Talbot "Tobe" Bateman in Fort Worth, William K. Patrick in many papers statewide, Hep Blackman in Fort Worth, Leo Cotton in San Antonio, Sam Kaiser in Houston, and Dennis McCarthy in Fort Worth.

The century's first decade was the last in which amateur cartoonists still held regular berths on the Texas newspapers—they were general-assignment newsroom staffers who did cartoons as a sideline, for the most part. The first-rate draftsmanship of Knott, Bateman, and increasingly the prolific Blessington raised the industry's standards for this specialized profession. These superior talents also received national exposure.

"Help!"
Cartoonist unknown
September 16, 1900
Houston Daily Post

At the dawn of the new century, Galveston suffered the greatest natural disaster ever to hit the United States. On September 8, 1900, a hurricane struck the Island City and killed six thousand of its citizens and impoverished more than 40 percent of those left alive. This appeal by a Denver artist for aid to hurricane victims was reprinted in the *Houston Daily Post*.

The citizens of Galveston rewrote the character of government to cope with the emergency. The Galveston Plan, or the concept of a city commission government, became the model adopted by many cities in the twentieth century. The city was rebuilt, including the still functional Sea Wall, in one of the greatest engineering feats of the new century. But Galveston never reclaimed its role as Texas' major port. Houston soon eclipsed the island in both population and economic importance.

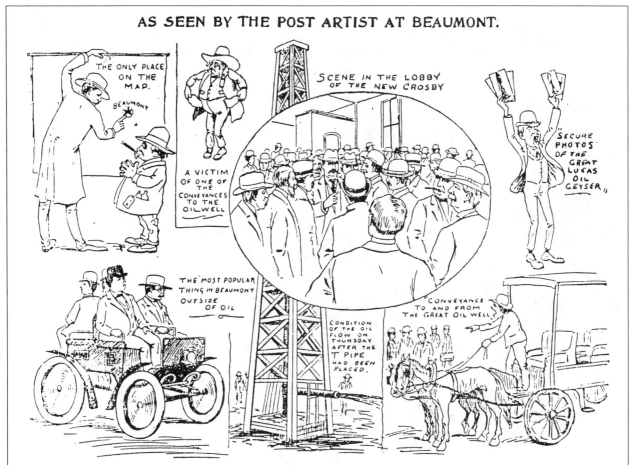

AS SEEN BY THE POST ARTIST AT BEAUMONT.

THE ONLY PLACE ON THE MAP.

BEAUMONT

A VICTIM OF ONE OF THE CONVEYANCES TO THE OIL WELL

SCENE IN THE LOBBY OF THE NEW CROSBY

"SECURE PHOTOS OF THE GREAT LUCAS OIL GEYSER"

THE MOST POPULAR THING IN BEAUMONT OUTSIDE OF OIL

CONDITION OF THE OIL FLOW ON THURSDAY AFTER THE T PIPE HAD BEEN PLACED.

CONVEYANCE TO AND FROM THE GREAT OIL WELL.

The sketches presented here depict some scenes at Beaumont as they appeared to a Post artist who spent a day viewing the oil geyser and the busy scenes incidental to the excitement over Captain Lucas' immense "spouter." The flow had been placed under control when The Post artist reached the well, but the excitement was by no means under control—no valve can be found strong enough to hold it. The crowds around the hotels give the town the appearance of a big convention center.

"As Seen . . . "
Cartoonist unknown
January 20, 1901
Houston Daily Post

The discovery of oil in Jefferson County signaled the birth of a major Texas industry and the breaking of Standard Oil's monopoly on production. Oil had been discovered in the state earlier, at Corsicana, but the largest well in the nation before 1901 produced only about 6,000 barrels per day. The well that came in on January 10, 1901, at Spindletop flowed between 70,000 and 100,000 barrels daily.

Speculators hurried to the Spindletop site. The *Post* artist depicts the frantic activities generated by wildcatter Capt. A. F. Lucas's discovery. In 1901, as a result of Spindletop, the state chartered 491 oil companies, which issued about $300 million of capital stock, or more than the total stock issued the previous decade.

THE PROBLEM AT AUSTIN.

"Taxation Bill"
Sam Kaiser
January 8, 1905
Houston Post

S. W. T. Lanham, who served as governor from 1903 to 1907, was not as progressive as James Hogg, but he did inherit the demands of agrarians that the state tax laws be revised. In 1905 the legislature set about making the tax laws more representative of the state's growing industrial potential. This cartoon shows the legislature puzzling over how to raise new taxes and at the same time switch the tax burden from simply a property tax to one that also would tax business. The result was a new franchise tax on companies' capital investments and taxes on intangible assets of corporations, as well as on the gross receipts of railroads and insurance corporations. A corporate income tax was introduced but failed to pass the legislature.

"SOME NEEDED LEGISLATION" WILL BE PROPOSED AT AUSTIN.

"Some Needed Legislation"
Sam Kaiser
January 10, 1905
Houston Post

The 1905 legislative session was a particularly stormy one. This pre-session cartoon predicted that legislators would arrive in Austin with numerous demands from their constituents for reform. In particular there were groundswells for revision of the tax laws. But moreover, Judge A. W. Terrell returned to the legislature promising new laws that would require primary elections for parties that polled more than one hundred thousand votes. The Terrell laws also set regular dates for primaries. In addition to taxes and election reform, the legislators in this image are holding bills that would regulate railroads, outlaw child labor, restrict banking, and forward other Progressive goals. Although the 1905 session fulfilled some major labor-union demands, among the bills that failed were those which would have restricted interest rates, created a pure food and drug regulatory commission, and begun water planning.

"Disfranchised!"
Tobe Bateman
January 29, 1905
Houston Post

The voting fraud of the 1890s and the argument that African-American participation in politics corrupted the Democratic party led reformers, conservatives, and ironically, some ex-Populists to endorse a poll tax as a proper method of voter registration. The Terrell Election Law of 1903 stipulated that poll taxes had to be paid between October and February to establish eligibility for voting the following November. The law also authorized a secret ballot and tried to bring some uniformity into the way that nominating conventions or primaries were held. The poll tax and the later all-white primaries eliminated much black participation in politics. Historians have estimated that only between 15,000 and 40,000 of the 160,000 African-American males over twenty-one in Texas retained the right to vote in 1920. The poll tax also disfranchised large numbers of poorer white voters, many of whom were former members of the Populist party.

BEGINNING TO SEE THROUGH NEW GLASSES.

"The Negro Question"
Cartoonist unknown
February 19, 1905
Houston Post

Southerners criticized Pres. Theodore Roosevelt for what they considered his sympathy for African Americans. Led by Sen. Joseph Bailey, Texans particularly objected to Roosevelt's decision to invite black educator Booker T. Washington to the White House for dinner. This cartoon celebrates what the artist considered a change in attitude that made Roosevelt more sympathetic to the white South. Indeed, the president would soon unfairly order that dishonorable discharges be given to a black regiment of troops, who while stationed at Brownsville, Texas, were erroneously charged with raiding that community after a series of clashes with civilians over discrimination.

"Come Across"
Tobe Bateman
April 7, 1906
Fort Worth Record

The 1890s had been marked by strikes and violence that swept the nation. Labor unrest, as the press described it, included also the use of federal or state authority to break the strikes. This cartoon salutes the move that began at the turn of the century to submit labor grievances to arbitration. Note the sun signaling the dawn of a new age, as the mine operator is invited to avoid the chasm of the strike.

TEXAS VOTERS:—"Say, but Won't the Capitol Loom Up With These New Trinkets?"

"Texas Voters"
Sam Kaiser
July 27, 1906
Houston Post

The gubernatorial contest of 1906 featured a campaign in which all candidates embraced Progressive measures. That summer the *Houston Post* endorsed O. B. Colquitt, who is shown here carrying his bags filled with Progressive reforms and headed to the state capital. However, in the first primary conducted under the new Terrell Election Law, Colquitt ran second to Thomas M. Campbell. Colquitt withdrew before the nominating convention, and Campbell became governor. Campbell was reelected in 1908, then chose not to run again. Among Campbell's accomplishments during his two terms in the statehouse were the enactment of utility regulation, passage of a pure-food law, strengthening of the state antitrust laws, and reform of the prison system. In addition, he attempted to control lobbyists and strengthened public education by providing more tax authority for local schools.

"Texas Industries"
Bert Blessington
January 20, 1907
Houston Post

Progressives believed in promoting business expansion and growth. This image celebrates the growth of Texas industry, which in 1906 reported the net worth of several firms of over $5 million in capitalization. The young state promises that as soon as the population expands, the market will encourage more economic growth. The state would not reach the magic five-million population mark, however, until after 1920.

THE FALLING OF A STAR—WITNESS

"The Falling of a Star"
Bert Blessington
February 1, 1907
Houston Post

Joseph Weldon Bailey was probably as controversial as any elected official in the state. He served in Congress from 1891 to 1901 and then in the U.S. Senate from 1901 to 1913. He voluntarily announced retirement in 1912 amid charges that he had been improperly hired, in what opponents described as an obvious conflict of interests, by both Standard Oil and Kirby Lumber Company to forward their causes in the state legislature.

A 1906 muckraking article in *Cosmopolitan* exposed U.S. senators' connections with large corporations, including those of Bailey. A 1907 legislative investigating committee exonerated Bailey of charges, but his opponents maintained that the committee had made a whitewash of the senator. This cartoon depicts the testimony of J. P. Gruett, Sr., who had stolen papers from the Waters-Pierce Oil Company and was the state's star witness.

"Showing up the Holes"
Tobe Bateman
February 8, 1908
Fort Worth Record

Democrats accused George B. Cortelyou of illegally forcing corporations to contribute to Theodore Roosevelt's 1904 campaign. Cortelyou became the secretary of the treasury, winning further Democratic hostility. His defense of Pres. Roosevelt's policies called forth a rebuttal by Culberson in the Senate. Culberson's attack on Cortelyou was widely praised by the press in Texas.

SENATOR BAILEY SHAKES THE ALDRICH BILL AND EXPOSES THE DETAILS.

"Senator Bailey"
Bert Blessington
March 10, 1908
Houston Post

On many political issues Joseph Weldon Bailey was an old-fashioned states' rights Democrat. He enlisted many Texas supporters who endorsed these views. Here, Bailey is shown advocating the traditional southern arguments against a proposal by Rhode Island senator Nelson Aldrich to expand paper currency to be guaranteed by bonds and issued by national banks, which were privately owned before the creation of the Federal Reserve System. Southerners traditionally wanted currency controlled by the government and not private enterprise. The Bailey proposal was defeated, and the Aldrich-Vreeland Act used private banks as issuers of capital.

"A Gentle Reminder"
Tobe Bateman
January 14, 1909
Fort Worth Record

White citizens of Brownsville resented the stationing of the 25th Infantry, composed entirely of African Americans, at Fort Brown. After several instances of conflict, whites charged that members of the unit raided the city and killed a white man. Pres. Theodore Roosevelt dismissed three companies stationed at Fort Brown when no soldier would testify as to the identity of the alleged culprits. A Senate committee investigated the incident and reported that no reliable information existed to connect the black troopers with the murder. In fact, the committee speculated that evidence pointed toward a frame-up involving a white saloon keeper or possibly smugglers who wished the troops removed. Nonetheless, the soldiers were not then reinstated. In this depiction, Roosevelt is confronted with the cover-up charges. The issue was one of many that cartoonist Bateman found sufficiently infuriating to provoke a pen-and-ink opinion: Because such outrages "got his goat," so to speak, Bateman introduced the wisecracking character at the lower right to illustrate his signature.

Cartoonists Find Their Role (1910–19)

In the second decade of the 1900s, Texas' concerns were increasingly of national significance. Perhaps most representative of this trend was the importance of the state's backstage political leader Col. Edward M. House as the shadowy *eminence grise* in Woodrow Wilson's administration—on Capitol Hill in domestic matters, and overseas at the Versailles Peace Conference. Itchy disputes with Mexico—from immigration problems to violent border raids to the Mexican government's perennial instability—garnered nationwide attention. So did Gov. James E. "Pa" Ferguson, a rough-speaking, self-styled commoner, whose efforts including rent-restriction schemes for impoverished farmers presaged Huey Long's Louisiana programs of the next generation, but who was derailed by a political smear campaign. Ferguson's wife, Miriam "Ma" Ferguson, would later become governor herself.

The Texan cartoonists found their work gracing the front pages with increasing frequency—and not merely because the issues were hotter. Artistic standards were rising, and the cartoonists were becoming influential commentators. Their distinctive identities were becoming more widely known, too: William K. Patrick's comical duck character prompted readers to refer to him as "the duck man," and Tobe Bateman's trademark mascot earned him recognition as "the goat." Patrick's gathering acclaim landed him local-issue cartooning assignments as far afield as New Orleans, where his contributions to the *Times-Picayune* included a striking commentary on the "Axeman" serial-murder case of 1918–19.

Bateman was a master at using exaggerated perspective for compelling effect, and his cagey placement of solid-black patches and intricate crosshatched shading served both to anchor a drawing on the page and to pull the reader's gaze straightaway to the target of ridicule. With ambitions to match his prolific output, Bateman ranged from Fort Worth (where, for a time, he worked simultaneously for Democrat and Republican dailies) to Dallas to San Antonio.

John Knott had joined the *Dallas News* in 1905, succeeding cartoonists named Scribner and Toomey, and remained there for decades; he also delivered gag panels for Hearst. However, he did not begin producing daily front-page editorial cartoons until late in 1911. By the time World War I broke out, Knott's popularity had soared, with the paper's circulation now approaching one hundred thousand. According to historian Gerald D. Saxon, "World War I unleashed a barrage of propaganda from both sides and it is not hyperbole to say the outcome of the war was influenced almost as much by cartoonists/propagandists like Knott as by the fighting on the Western and Eastern fronts."

Jack Patton was enrolled at the Academy of fine Arts in Chicago in 1918 when he received word that the old *Dallas Journal*, the evening publication of the *Dallas News*, needed an assistant in the art department. Hurrying back to his hometown, Patton found to his delight that he would be working with the veteran Knott. Two years later his editorial cartoons won a place on page 1 of the *Journal*. He became one of the few artists in the business to put out both an editorial cartoon and a daily comic strip. In Houston, the *Post*'s Bert Blessington elevated his profile by delivering chalk-talks to schools and illustrating election-night news on projection screens.

The Whole State Knows at Last

ANNOUNCING HIS INTENTION

"The Whole State Knows at Last"
Tobe Bateman
July 8, 1910
Daily Express

Joseph Bailey endorsed William Poindexter in the 1910 gubernatorial campaign rather than Cone Johnson, an old Bailey foe. Poindexter was a moderate dry; he and Johnson, a vigorous foe of liquor, split the prohibitionist forces in the 1910 nominating convention and allowed Oscar Branch Colquitt—who supported local option but not statewide Prohibition—to capture the nomination and the election as governor.

"Trying to Find a Place to Put It"
Tobe Bateman
July 15, 1910
Daily Express

The Anti-Saloon League came to Texas in 1907 and worked to create a coalition of dry forces that would break a stalemate with the Texas Brewers Association, which financed wet political campaigns. These "drys" campaigned for a 1910 amendment to the Texas Constitution that would outlaw liquor statewide in a single vote (thus bypassing the opposition to Prohibition in the Hill Country and South Texas). This anti-prohibitionist cartoon takes the view of San Antonio's wet interests in depicting the demand for the constitutional amendment as a fifth wheel.

"Toot Toot"
Heppner Blackman
January 15, 1911
Brenham Daily News

Thomas B. Campbell's gubernatorial victory in 1906 was considered an endorsement of Progressive reform. Indeed, much praiseworthy activity distinguished his two administrations, including the establishment of a Department of Agriculture, laws restricting free passes on railroads, and insurance and banking legislation. Critics maintained, however, that Campbell was not a sufficiently forceful leader. This lampoon shows the governor giving an indecisive and cliché-ridden speech as he voluntarily retires. He holds a plank from his failed platform. At his feet are rumors of scandals involving his administration. Charges of nepotism in the Texas Rangers and appointed offices are represented by the gun in his pocket and the "son-in-law" commission on the depot's porch.

"Make the Scales Balance"
W. K. Patrick
November 1, 1911
Fort Worth Record

Periodically trade conferences were called in the South to improve conditions for cotton farmers and to raise their prices. In the fall of 1911, such a conference met in New Orleans. Governor Colquitt attended the conference and expressed confidence in its outcome. Among the proposals were changes in the national tariff policy, restrictions on cotton speculators, and other government measures to aid embattled farmers. This image urges Uncle Sam to enact measures, as recommended by the southern governors, which would increase cotton consumption and help counterbalance overproduction. It repeats, by implication, the historic charge that the federal government favored manufacturing interests at the expense of southern farmers: hence the cotton scales as a symbol and the words "tote fair," voiced by cartoonist Patrick's now-familiar duck character in rustic vernacular.

As Chairman of the Penitentiary Board He Did Not Make a Move to Abolish the Inhuman Bat.

"As Chairman . . . "
Bert Blessington
July 24, 1912
Houston Post

Prison conditions and reform have been a never-ending point of controversy in Texas history. A series of newspaper articles in 1908 and 1909 exposed deplorable prison conditions and the horrors of the convict-lease system in Texas. A special legislative session in 1910 mandated a gradual phasing-out of the convict-leasing program, as well as some other moderate reforms, but allowed the continuation of whipping as punishment. The legislature authorized a three-man penitentiary board to be appointed by the governor. This 1912 image criticizes W. F. Ramsey, the board chairman, for allowing the use of the "bat," or prison whip. Convict leasing ended later that year, but constant charges of mismanagement of prisons and prison revenue surfaced with regularity through 1925. In that year, a constitutional amendment was ratified that authorized a reorganization of the management and supervision of the prison system.

TAX EATERS vs. TAX PAYERS

MR. COLQUITT HAS DRAWN FROM THE STATE TREASURY TWENTY-EIGHT THOUSAND DOLLARS DURING THE PAST SEVEN YEARS. DURING THAT TIME HE HAS NOT CONTRIBUTED ENOUGH TO THE SUPPORT OF THE STATE TO PAY THE TUITION OF HIS OWN CHILDREN.

"Tax Eaters . . . "
Cartoonist unknown
Circa 1912
Publication unknown

Governor Colquitt faced opposition for his re-election in 1912 from Progressives who identified him as wrong on Prohibition and not a strong enough supporter of Woodrow Wilson. Certainly Colquitt was more conservative than his predecessor, but he was not the arch reactionary that his detractors would have had the voters believe. He did inherit a deficit in the state treasury, and that plus his determination to run a frugal government and his natural conservatism led him to veto several fiscal measures. Among those laws which he opposed were free distribution of textbooks in the public schools, some appropriations for the state university, and higher salaries for public school teachers. The latter issue is the subject for this cartoon, found in the collection of the Barker Texas History Center at the University of Texas, in which Colquitt is depicted as one who lives off public salary, while underpaid school teachers are ignored. The bottle in Colquitt's pocket symbolizes his opposition to Prohibition.

"Fill in the Gaps"
Heppner Blackman
January 13, 1913
Brenham Daily News

By 1913 many of the state's railroads were near bankruptcy, partially because of stock watering, and repairs and new construction had ended. A report of needed measures to help Texas industrialize said that manufacturing capacity and new plants had grown so during the last twenty years that transportation facilities were no longer adequate. The stock requirements for financing repairs and expansion of railroads depended on the Railroad Commission and its evaluation of the financial stability of the road. Critics of Governor Hogg's 1893 Stock and Bond Law argued that a key requirement—that new railroad securities could not exceed the Railroad Commission's evaluation of a line's property—made it impossible to raise capital. This cartoon shows a pile of crossties representing amendments needed to overcome the old Hogg law.

"What Ferguson Victory Will Mean"
Burt Blessington
June 18, 1914
Houston Telegram

Jim Ferguson burst upon the political scene in 1914. A self-made man, he announced his candidacy for governor, citing the need for a businessman in office. Among his campaign promises was legislation to prevent landlords from collecting more than one-fourth of the value of a tenant farmer's cotton crop and one-third of the value of the grain crop. Ferguson counted on farmers' votes in North and East Texas to make him governor. Moreover, his rhetoric and demeanor won the hearts of many rural Texans. They called him "Farmer Jim" and "Pa," and his folksy speech and deliberately faulty grammar kept many of them entranced for the next twenty-five years. He defeated Thomas Ball from Houston by more than forty thousand votes in the primary and won the November general election by a substantial margin. As governor, he passed in his first administration legislation restricting farm rents, but not much effort was put into enforcement. The U. S. Supreme Court declared the act unconstitutional in 1921.

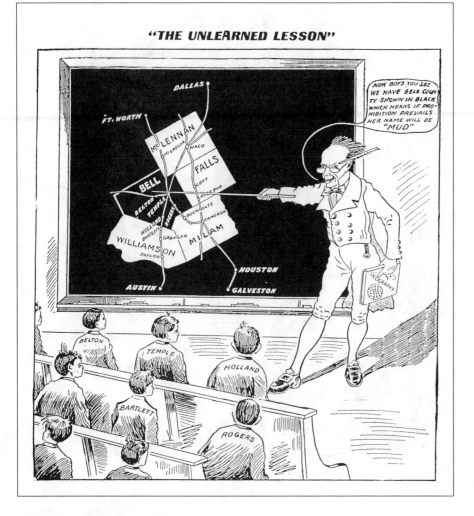

"The Unlearned Lesson"
Cartoonist unknown
November 7, 1915
Temple Mirror

Even though the 1910 campaign for statewide Prohibition had failed, local option elections continued. This cartoon warns that if a county votes a local option law, business will go elsewhere. This argument was an effective strategy for the wet forces. Prohibition came to Texas with the legislature's ratification of the Eighteenth Amendment to the U.S. Constitution on February 28, 1918.

"Why She Is a Wall Flower"
John Knott
June 7, 1917
Dallas Morning News

World War I was financed partially by the sale of liberty bonds. When the war began, investors discovered that private securities paid more interest than public investments did. Texas capitalists are depicted here as waltzing away with better returns and neglecting public bonds.

John Knott's reputation was built on cartoons that he drew about World War I. From the outbreak of the war in Europe in 1914 to the signing of the Treaty of Versailles, Knott brought the war to people's living rooms. The *Hillsboro Mirror* referred to him as that "splendid cartoonist who helped win the war. His pictures increased the purchase of Liberty Bonds, and ran up the contributions to the Red Cross, Salvation Army, or Y.M.C.A."

THE NEW FLY-SWATTER

"The New Fly-Swatter"
John Knott
May 9, 1918
Dallas Morning News

The first World War was also the first war in which all civilians had to be enlisted in an all-out military and industrial effort. Immigration had increased the ethnic diversity of the nation. Anxious to bring about support for total war from all the ethnic groups, the U.S. government unleashed a propaganda barrage. State governments joined in the effort. Texas, for example, made it punishable by imprisonment to make negative public remarks on the war effort, the flag, military uniforms, or the U.S. government. This cartoon encourages Congress to pass the Sedition Bill, which would provide severe penalties for anyone condemning the war effort or the flag or using "disloyal, scurrilous or abusive" language concerning the government, the Constitution, or the military forces. The act was passed seven days after the cartoon saw print. The Sedition Act was used primarily to suppress socialists, labor union organizers, and radical organizations.

ONE MORE COOK OUGHT TO IMPROVE THE BROTH

"One More Cook Ought to Improve the Broth"
John Knott
July 10, 1918
Dallas Morning News

Woman's suffrage was another Progressive goal that was accomplished as a result of World War I. Women had organized the Texas Woman Suffrage Association in 1903. The organization petitioned the legislature in 1907 and 1913 for the right to vote. Male opposition defeated the proposals. But the participation of the organization in the Ferguson impeachment campaign and the service of women in World War I lessened opposition. In a special session in 1918, the legislature extended to women the right to vote in primary elections.

This cartoon welcomes the new woman voter. She is going to clean up the kitchen of dirty politics. It is also important to compare her image with the earlier portrayal of suffragettes. Note that she is now clearly an attractive, middle-class woman who represents mainstream Progressive values, unlike her portrayal in the cartoon of June 17, 1894.

"Mud"
John Knott
July 19, 1918
Dallas Morning News

This cartoon shows ex-governor James E. "Pa" Ferguson throwing mud in his continuing attack on the University of Texas. This fight began during his second term, when he tried to force the Board of Regents to fire certain faculty members and, when the board refused, vetoed virtually the entire appropriation for the university. The battle over the University of Texas united Progressives in their determination to remove Governor Ferguson from office. In the summer of 1917 impeachment charges were drawn up. Ferguson resigned rather than be expelled from public office. The court of impeachment acted anyway, denying him the right to hold office again. Ferguson maintained that he could hold public office since he had resigned before he was expelled, and he challenged William P. Hobby in the 1918 gubernatorial campaign. During his campaign, he continued to attack the university. Hobby won the primary by more than two hundred thousand votes.

Roaring into the Twenties (1920–29)

As America emerged from the Great War, an intensifying national attitude was crystallized in a popular song that asked, "How You Gonna Keep 'Em Down on the Farm (After They've Seen Paree)?" The line was no mere Tin Pan Alley "hook," but rather the lyrical equivalent of an editorial cartoon—voicing a concern over the rural regions' gathering abandonment.

But the Texans, characteristically a maverick breed predisposed to the bucking of trends, did come home: There was work to be done, thanks to economic upheavals that had as much to do with the countryside as with the cities. The Lone Star State shared in the general prosperity of the country. The oil business was booming, and the state's population was expanding proportionately faster than the nation's because of the workers attracted to the fields and factories.

Cultural upheavals abounded, as well. Evolution in education was literally that, what with a persistent campaign to bar the teaching of Darwinism. And Texas was bracing to make revolutionary contributions to popular music. The celebrated white southern blues singer Jimmie Rodgers became a frequent visitor, catalyzing a 1929 fusion of jazz and country that would become known as Western swing under Texas bandleaders Milton Brown and Bob Wills. Meanwhile, African-American guitarist Blind Lemon Jefferson was coming to prominence around Dallas; white Texas' Western swing would feel his influence, too.

It was a memorable decade for cartooning. The twenties saw not only the inauguration of the Pulitzer Prize for cartooning—granting the political 'toon distinction as much in society at large as in the journalistic profession—but also the birth of such iconic characters as Popeye the Sailor and Mickey Mouse. There was a nationwide explosion of interest in social commentary and satire; the magazine *College Humor* had its start as the decade dawned, and *Ballyhoo*, an ancestor of *MAD* magazine, arrived at the close of the twenties.

Of Texas' native cartoonists, John Knott made the decade virtually his own. True, there were fewer Lone Star cartoonists than in other periods—but Knott would have dominated his field in any event. The twenties saw his style mature, his ideas gain strength and focus, to a point where Knott was routinely reprinted in such mass-market publications as *Cartoons* magazine and the *Literary Digest*.

Knott drew in a realistically humorous style, infusing his scenarios with the same sort of droll, antic wit that can be found in Will Rogers's motion-picture comedies of the same period. But like Rogers, Knott used the playful approach as a vehicle for barbed, earnest commentary. Like the eastern cartoonists of the Social Realist school, Knott often deepened his pen-and-ink compositions with bold grease-crayon chiaroscuro, attaining an unrivaled level of sophistication.

Knott's trademark character became a standard-bearer for the state. The Republicans had their elephant, the Democrats their donkey; the United States as a whole was represented by Uncle Sam. Knott gave Texas a comparable emblem in his figure of an old-school stalwart with broad-brimmed hat, flowing white moustache, string tie, and planter's vest. Knott's Old Man Texas became known throughout the nation.

But Knott was hardly the only name in Texas cartooning of the twenties. The wide-ranging Talbot "Tobe" Bateman joined the *Dallas News* in 1921 and became art director in 1925. Bert Blessington remained a mainstay at the *Post* in Houston, where he sidelined as a news photographer and performed community-service demonstrations of his hard-hitting political artistry.

Jack Patton gathered momentum in Dallas, making history even as he documented history. As a sideline to his editorial panels, Patton teamed with writer John Rosenfield, Jr., in 1926 to produce the *News* strip called *Texas History Movies*. This series traced state history in seriocomic fashion starting in 1493, when Christopher Columbus presented Indians and new world treasures to the Spanish Court. Abiding as a Texas classroom fixture into the 1960s, a book version of *Texas History Movies* would prove a deciding factor in shaping the careers of such currently significant players as the "underground" cartoonist and historian Jack "Jaxon" Jackson and the *Austin American-Statesman*'s Ben Sargent.

Another busy cartoonist, William K. Patrick, settled in at the *San Antonio Express* in 1924, there to remain until his death in 1936. The upstart in this community was V. T. Hamlin, who burst into print at the *Fort Worth Star-Telegram* with an ambitious variety of humor-strip, sports-commentary, and editorial cartoons. Hamlin would find a truer calling in the 1930s as a creator of the long-running syndicated strip *Alley Oop*.

"COME OUT AND BE COUNTED"

"Come Out and Be Counted"
John Knott
January 6, 1920
Dallas Morning News

The Texas media predicted that the 1920 U.S. Census would report that the population of the state exceeded 5,000,000. This cartoon shows Uncle Sam knocking at Texas' door, eagerly anticipating the response. To the disappointment of the state's leaders, the population total counted in at about 4,650,000. Most of those Texans resided in rural areas and were either Lone Star natives or immigrants from nearby southern states.

"The Innocent Bystander"
John Knott
June 5, 1920
Dallas Morning News

Among the strikes that swept the nation during 1919–20 were those of the longshoremen in major ports. In the summer of 1920 a walkout in Galveston tied up the shipping of Texas cotton. The general attitude that labor unions interfered with the economic development of the state is represented by Knott's depiction of Old Man Texas as outraged and frustrated by the strike's interruption of commerce. Pat Neff, the governor, was so unsympathetic toward labor that he would use martial law to stop a railroad strike the next year at Denison. That and other pro-management statements on his part led organized labor to oppose him in 1922. He won handily.

"The Fence Would Be Perfectly Tight..."
John Knott
January 7, 1921
Dallas Morning News

The Emergency Quota Act, or the Johnson Act, of 1921 provided that the annual immigration of any given nationality could not exceed 3 percent of the number of immigrants from that nation residing in the United States in 1910. The act did not satisfy the proponents of restricted immigration. This cartoon objects to leaving the doors open to immigrants from the Western Hemisphere. The act would be amended in 1927 to set a limit of 150,000 immigrants each year. The new act would virtually eliminate all immigrants from Asia and sharply curtail immigration from Southern and Eastern Europe. Immigrants from the Western Hemisphere would still be exempted under the 1927 legislation, however. Soon Mexicans and Puerto Ricans would become the largest group of newcomers to the continental United States.

"Good Luck"
John Knott
January 18, 1921
Dallas Morning News

Pat Neff entered the gubernatorial primary race in 1919 as a prohibitionist who supported Pres. Woodrow Wilson. Joe Bailey ran against Neff, denouncing almost all of the Progressive goals of the preceding decade. Wilsonian Progressives rallied to Neff's cause. Bailey led in the first primary in 1920 but lost the runoff. Neff's victory was hailed as a welcome triumph by the *Dallas Morning News* and by the Mexican government, which believed that the new governor would endorse free trade and be more sympathetic to the revolution than had some earlier governors.

"Red River Boundary Dispute"
John Knott
Circa 1922
Dallas Morning News

When oil was discovered in the bed of the Red River in 1919, Texas claimed the southern half of the river, and its oilmen began to drill. However, Oklahoma claimed the whole riverbed on the basis of a Supreme Court decision made in 1896, and Oklahoma oilmen also began to work the southern half of the river. Armed conflict threatened, and Oklahoma took the case to the Supreme Court. To complicate matters, the U.S. government claimed the southern half of the river as a trustee for the Indians of Oklahoma! Though Old Man Texas may think he has Oklahoma cornered, the Supreme Court in 1923 gave Oklahoma political control of the entire riverbed. In addition, the court made the United States the trustee for the Indians and awarded them the rights to oil in the southern half of the riverbed.

A KLANSMAN'S CREED

FOR
Sanctity of Home
white Supremacy
Free Public Schools
belonging to State
Purity in Politics
Christian Religion
Bible
Constituted Authority
Limited Foreign Immi-
gration.
Law and Order
Charity, Love and
Character.
Purity of Woman-
Hood. God
America. Always.

AGAINST
Trouble-making
Wrong-doing.
Foreign-domination.
Vatican Control of
America.
Flogging.
Tar and Feathers.
Ruin-degradation.
Bootleggery
Unjust Treatment

"A Klansman's Creed"
Cartoonist unknown
June 9, 1922
Texas 100 Per Cent American

The Ku Klux Klan appeared in Texas in 1921, billing itself as a proponent of white Protestantism and a protector of the state from declining morals. The organization was able to play on the fears of rural Americans, who saw the failure of urban America to enforce Prohibition as an example of declining Anglo-Saxon values. The Klan was anti-foreign and excluded both Jews and Catholics from membership.

The Klansman in this sympathetic cartoon, published in the Klan's own newspaper, denies that the Klan sanctions violence and is careful to point out that it opposes immigration, supports patriotism, and wishes to uphold law and order.

"Mud-Slinging 'Jimmie' Ferguson"
Collins
August 11, 1922
Texas 100 Per Cent American

The Klan candidate in the 1922 U.S. senatorial election was Earle B. Mayfield. "Farmer Jim" Ferguson denied that the earlier state actions that prevented him from running for governor made him ineligible for the U.S. Senate. Mayfield won the election over Ferguson, with the reluctant support of many of the old Progressives, who saw the Klansman as the lesser evil. This cartoon tries to entice Progressive support by depicting Mayfield as a principled sort, declining to stoop to the gutter tactics used by the profane Ferguson. Note also the "I want light wine," remark, which attempts to identify Ferguson once more with liquor interests.

"Git Away from There"
John Knott
January 21, 1923
Dallas Morning News

In 1923 a bill was introduced in the Texas Legislature to bar the teaching of evolution in any state-supported educational institution. It passed the House but died in the Senate. The next year another version, which would have fired teachers and restricted textbooks that taught evolution, was sent to the floor of the legislature. It also failed, but similar bills were debated in each session until 1929. Several southern states passed such legislation. But in Texas, despite pressure from such lobbying groups as the Texas Sunday School Association, the legislature did not pass an anti-evolution law. Historians cite the heterogeneity of the state's population and the opposition to such legislation from the Hill Country and South Texas as reasons the proposals failed.

"Help Needed"
John Knott
January 25, 1923
Dallas Morning News

The pink or Mexican cotton bollworm was reported in Midland and Ector counties in the winter of 1928. It was the second time within ten years that the pest had appeared outside the Big Bend. The farmers asked that the federal government join with state authorities and eradicate the pest before it could infect more crops. It was traditional that nearby agricultural states would demand a quarantine on Texas cotton if massive intervention did not occur. Although not as destructive as the boll weevil, the bollworm continued to spread despite federal and state actions. As late as 1952 the insect destroyed $28 million worth of cotton. The pink bollworm was eventually controlled by a combination of early strains of hybrid cotton, new methods of cultivation, and the use of insecticides.

The Favorite Campaign Dodger of the Anti-Klan Forces—Mrs. Ferguson Standing Behind the Constitution—The Little Man Kneeling Before the Masked Knight Is Robertson, the K. K. K. Candidate.

"Constitution and By-Laws of the Ku Klux Klan"
Cartoonist unknown
August, 1924
Dallas Morning News

The 1924 campaign for governor featured as a principal issue the Ku Klux Klan. The growth of violence associated with the Klan disillusioned many of its former supporters, who had overlooked its xenophobia and religious intolerance and focused on the Klan's alleged opposition to bootlegging. Miriam "Ma" Ferguson challenged the Klan candidate, Felix D. Robertson, in the Democratic primary. She ran as a defender of constitutionalism in opposition to Klan violence. She also usually closed her campaign by noting that a vote for her was also a vote for "Pa" Ferguson.

The Klan in turn depicted Miriam Ferguson as a front for "Farmer" Jim and the liquor interests. Many of the former Progressive Democrats did not know where to go. Most reluctantly supported "Ma," who won the primary, but then they backed George C. Butte, who garnered a rather spectacular 300,000 votes as a Republican. Mrs. Ferguson, however, won with more than 400,000 and became the first woman governor of Texas.

"The Hungry Razorback"
John Knott
February 26, 1925
Dallas Morning News

The prison system emerged as an issue again in the 1920s. The idea behind prison farms was that they would be self-sufficient. That turned out, of course, not to be the case. Texas is shown in this cartoon as attempting to understand why the system would cost taxpayers a million dollars a year. Frustration with the prison system would lead in 1925 to ratification of a constitutional amendment that authorized a reorganization of the management and supervision of the prison system. Shortly thereafter the Texas Prison Board was created. Controversies did not end.

"Ma Holds Off the Calf . . . "
Cartoonist unknown
May, 1926
Free Lance

Miriam Ferguson's administration was a controversial one, with scandals over the granting of pardons and the letting of highway contracts. Opponents maintained that she was a token leader of the state and that her husband was running the state for the benefit of special interests. The administration was also under fire for not cutting taxes, as had been promised, and for failure to reform public schools.

"Fergusonism . . . "
Bert Blessington
May 29, 1926
Free Lance

Governor Ferguson had promised to be a one-term governor but changed her mind and announced her intention to run in the 1926 campaign. Progressive Democrats endorsed Dan Moody, the attorney general in the Ferguson administration, to run against the incumbent. Moody ran a hard-hitting campaign which opened with a May speech at Georgetown that accused the Fergusons of corruption. He defeated "Ma" Ferguson by more than 200,000 votes in the 1926 runoff.

He Should Carry the Solid South on This Platform

"He Should Carry the Solid South on This Platform"
John Knott
January 31, 1928
Dallas Morning News

Having defeated Miriam Ferguson, Dan Moody went on to become one of the most popular governors in the state's history. He was quickly recognized by the national media as a spokesman for the South. Moody proposed in 1928 that the South limit the production of cotton by legislative action. The plan went nowhere, but it garnered Moody abundant national publicity. As the presidential nominating convention for the Democratic party neared that year, Progressive southerners sent up trial balloons for the nomination of Moody for either president or vice-president on the Democratic ticket. The plan went awry. Moody, to the distaste of some of the other Progressive southerners, supported Al Smith's nomination for president. Many of Moody's peers, however, bolted the party, citing Smith's opposition to Prohibition as making him unworthy of their support. Smith lost Texas, and Moody won re-election to the governor's office in 1928.

"Over the Jumps"
Bert Blessington
June 26, 1928
Houston Post

The Democratic party in 1928 was divided between its various factions, with the Northeast urging the nomination of Al Smith of New York and the South wishing a candidate more attuned to rural values. At the national Democratic party nominating convention, which met in Houston that year, party chairman Clem Shaver of West Virginia tried to prevent the Democrats from dividing as they had in 1924 over the issues of Prohibition and the Klan. This cartoon warns that Shaver will have a tough time taking the Democratic donkey over the jumps that divided the party—sectionalism and the old factionalism that had weakened the party in both 1920 and 1924. The Democrats nominated Smith, and the South voted Republican for the first time since 1868.

"The Strong Man Act"
Harold Cargill
November 20, 1928
Houston Chronicle

Herbert Hoover won the presidential election in 1928, defeating Democrat Al Smith. The Republicans spoke of finally breaking the "solid South." Since the southern states had cast their electoral votes for Hoover, the G.O.P. hoped that the former Confederate states would no longer automatically vote for Democratic presidential and congressional candidates. The cartoonist drew an image of a Republican party appearing to hoist up the southern states' electoral vote, but with Hoover's popularity supplying the real strength. Actually Texas' vote for Hoover was a vote for prosperity and against Smith, who was both a "wet" and a Catholic. Texans would not again cast a majority vote for a Republican presidential candidate until 1952.

Times of Bust and Dust (1930–39)

The Great Depression of the 1930s was a time when every nuance of the news took on a paramount importance to everyday folk. People demanded their news, whether the topic was the general worsening of economic fortunes, gathering war clouds overseas, or, in Texas, the close-to-home Dust Bowl crisis that sent masses of hard-pressed rural Oklahomans migrating westward in search of work. This popular obsession with information placed a special responsibility on the political cartoonists as interpreters and commentators. The profession gained intense momentum in Texas, where metropolitan-area newspapers had long since learned the circulation-building value of resident cartoonists.

The development of local cartooning can be seen as a side-effect of an overall explosion in popular culture, a mingled function of art and commerce that such essayists as Frederick Nye and James Sallis have perceptively defined as history in caricature. Hard times invariably stimulate an appetite for entertainment, and the cartoonists—an aggressive lot to begin with—responded as energetically to the depression as the music and motion-picture industries.

As cartooning blossomed in Texas, so did the native Texan musical idiom known as Western swing. A prominent supporter of both movements was W. Lee "Pappy" O'Daniel, Light Crust Flour magnate and radio pitchman, front man for the Light Crust Doughboys swing band—and, as of 1938, governor of Texas. A businessman whose calculatedly folksy image provoked detractors to complain that he "peddled politics like biscuits," O'Daniel also was an enthusiastic follower of the cartoon community, adorning his office with many original drawings. However, while O'Daniel loved the cartoon community, their affection for him was often drawn in cynical terms. John Knott never understood O'Daniel and was said to be repulsed by his hillbilly character. Knott felt he had no sense of politics but was just a flour salesman out to get votes.

Busiest of Texas' cartoonists—and likely, the most popularly beloved—was Jack Patton, whose increasingly cheeky editorial commentaries bespoke a refusal to loaf on the laurels of his humorous and history-oriented strip-format cartoons. By the thirties, the *Dallas News* strip, *Texas History Movies*, by Jack Patton and John Rosenfield, Jr., had become an institution. Begun in 1926 and first collected in book form in 1928, the seriocomic documentary feature figured in the education of three generations of Texans, with hundreds of thousands of copies distributed over the long stretch.

Patton's pen-and-ink style, distinguished by an exaggerated realism carried over from the comic strips, took shape while he was a student at the Chicago Academy of fine Arts. Indeed, Patton's compositions and figures resemble the "Chicago look" of such contemporaries as W. A. "Wally" Carlson (of *The Nebbs* and *Mostly Malarkey*) and Jimmy Murphy (of *Toots & Casper*)—a stylistic heritage that remains vivid in Chicagoan Jay Lynch's *Phoebe & the Pigeon People* strips of recent years. If the style was an acquired one for Patton, he made it thoroughly his own with a sharp eye for accurate caricature, a briskness of line and striking shadowplay, and a gift for applying metaphorical absurdities to Texas' political concerns. Patton was a respected, prolific mainstay of the *News* at the time of his death in 1962.

M. A. Dunning drew for the *Austin American-Statesman* beginning in 1938 following hitches with the *Houston Post*, the *San Diego Tribune*, and the *Atlanta Constitution*. Master of a humorous style reflecting the influence of Carey Orr in Chicago and Billy Ireland of Columbus, Ohio, Dunning was widely reprinted. The motion implicit in his panels gives away his early work in the studios of embittered rivals Charles Mintz (*Krazy Kat* and *Scrappy*) and Walt Disney; Dunning's Disney assignments included contributions to the watershed cartoon *The Three Little Pigs*.

Hal Coffman was a cartoonist of national prominence when he joined the *Fort Worth Star-Telegram* in 1939. He brought a significant national-scene perspective to Texas cartooning, gracing the Fort Worth daily pages with interpretations of issues that embraced but also transcended regional concerns. He had drawn for papers in Los Angeles, Philadelphia, and New York—in New York for the flagship Hearst paper, the *American*, where Coffman had shared editorial-page space with the legendary Winsor McCay and illustrated the essays of Arthur Brisbane. Coffman's powerful images graced the Fort Worth newspaper for sixteen years, when he retired. *Star-Telegram* publisher Amon G. Carter, a prominent art connoisseur who established the definitive collections of Frederick Remington and Charles Russell, declared Coffman to be "a philosopher with an artistic mind."

Coffman was a friendly character who, rumor has it, used to hide a bottle of liquor in the trash basket next to his desk. Carter, the rumor continued, would come around each morning and take it out of his trash and not return it to him until the day's cartoon was complete. It was a wonderful relationship between publisher and cartoonist which lasted until the latter's death.

And not to overlook the obvious, Dallas's John Knott remained a vivid presence during the thirties, his cartoons taking on a (perhaps premature) statesmanlike dignity in sharp contrast to Jack Patton's increasingly rambunctious panels.

THE BOOK OF TRADITIONS

"Present School System"
T. Chambers
March, 1930
Texas Outlook

The Great Depression dominated the 1930s with demands that public institutions be reformed to operate more efficiently. This cartoon suggests that it is time to close the book on the old Texas school system and create a new one. Among the proposals were that schools stay open all year long, that buildings be adapted to multiple uses, and that schoolteachers and administrators be twelve-month state employees.

"Not What It's Cracked Up to Be"
Tobe Bateman
August 8, 1930
Dallas Morning News

Gov. Dan Moody chose not to seek re-election in 1930. Miriam Ferguson decided to run again. So did fifteen others, among them Ross Sterling, a successful oil entrepreneur from Houston. The *Dallas Morning News* saw the Ferguson campaign as a reprise of the "rotten egg" situation of 1924. Nevertheless, Mrs. Ferguson led in the first primary, then lost to Sterling in the runoff. Sterling had promised a businesslike approach to running the state government. Significantly, neither candidate made any proposals about how to meet the current economic crisis. Note that cartoonist Bateman's trademark goat character has been replaced by a cat.

"The Shadow"
John Knott
February 25, 1931
Dallas Morning News

The crises of the thirties worsened. This cartoon is one of the few of the period to note that African Americans and whites shared the problem of destitution. Knott here depicts a failed economy, which casts a plague on whites and gives them a new, if shadowy, relationship with the black poor.

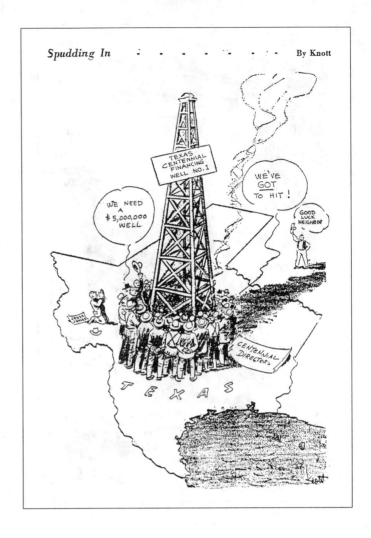

"Spudding In"
John Knott
March 16, 1931
Dallas Morning News

The state began in 1931 to plan for the 1936 celebration of the Texas Centennial. Jesse Jones, an entrepreneur from Houston who won considerable notoriety in the Franklin Roosevelt administrations, was originally in charge of rallying business interests for the 1936 extravaganza, for which the State Fair in Dallas would be the centerpiece. The promise was that investment in a series of celebrations around the state would help counteract the depression. A vote for a state constitutional amendment to support bonds for the celebration was slated for 1932. Jones resigned as centennial chief later in 1931 to serve the Hoover administration as director of the Reconstruction Finance Corporation.

"His Burden"
Tobe Bateman
August 13, 1931
Dallas Morning News

Falling prices in 1931 brought the price of cotton to below six cents per pound. In addition, a bumper crop, including more than 5 million bales produced by Texas farmers, and an excess of unsold 1930 cotton, threatened to drive prices yet lower. The surplus prompted southern governors to meet in Austin to encourage a measure to restrict planting. Most favored state legislation that would limit acreage. Texas passed such a law, which restricted 1932 cotton to about 30 percent of that which had been planted in 1931. Governor Sterling was not enthusiastic about enforcing the provisions, and the U.S. Supreme Court would later strike the law down.

"Can He Sell the Old Man?"
John Knott
January 3, 1932
Dallas Morning News

John Nance Garner, who in 1931 became the first Texan ever elected speaker of the U.S. House of Representatives, proposed that year that Texas consider dividing itself into five states. Texas has such a right, by terms of the treaty by which the Republic joined the union and the Compromise of 1850. Garner probably was not serious in his proposal, but he pointed out that such an action would increase Texans' representation in the U.S. Senate. Proposals of this nature have been offered from the time of Reconstruction to the present day.

GOOD WORK SON, YOU'LL DO

"Good Work, Son, You'll Do"
Sam Kiser
May 5, 1932
Houston Post

John Nance Garner went to the Democratic convention in 1932 with the votes of both the Texas and California delegations. In this image, he is congratulated for tying up the California delegation. At the convention, Garner eventually threw his support and delegates to Franklin D. Roosevelt, who in turn selected the Texan as the vice-presidential nominee. Garner became, thus, the first Texan to serve as vice-president of the United States. Artist Kiser's adaptation of John Knott's Old Man Texas character demonstrates Knott's immense influence.

Election Ups and Downs · · · · · · · —By Bateman

"Election Ups and Downs"
Tobe Bateman
August 30, 1932
Fort Worth Star-Telegram

The two front-runners in the 1930 governor's race were Miriam Ferguson and Ross S. Sterling, former president of Mobil Oil. Sterling won the office. Ferguson decided to challenge Sterling to a rematch in 1932. The election was fraught with charges of fraud. Ferguson won, with a slim margin of 4,000 votes out of more than 950,000 ballots. Vote totals exceeded poll-tax receipts in some of the East Texas counties where the Fergusons had strong political support. Sterling filed a suit contesting Mrs. Ferguson's nomination as the Democratic party candidate. The Texas Supreme Court ruled that her name could go on the general election ballot, and she defeated Republican Orville Bullington in November.

The China Shop — — — — — — — By Jack Patton
—Journal Staff Artist.

"The China Shop"
Jack Patton
January 12, 1933
Dallas Journal

The second administration of Miriam Ferguson (1933–35) began with the state facing a financial catastrophe of a $14 million debt and a failed welfare system. Governor Ferguson and the legislature sparred over the issue of taxes. The governor proposed a sales tax and some corporate and income taxes. The sales tax was particularly controversial. In this cartoon "Ma" and "Pa" Ferguson are seen leading the sales-tax "bull" into a china shop, representing business-industrial interests, with the implicit message that the tax would destroy the shop for all members of society. The sales tax failed to pass. The legislature instead passed a small per-barrel levy on oil.

"Maybe This Will Hold Him for a While"
Jack Patton
April 25, 1933
Dallas Journal

In October, 1930, Columbus Marion "Pop" Joiner drilled an oil well near Kilgore and hit the great East Texas field. The immense find drove the price of oil down from a dollar a barrel to eight cents in 1931. Consequently, the Texas Railroad Commission issued proration orders for East Texas to restrict the pumping of oil. Some operators procured injunctions to prevent the Railroad Commission from limiting production. Others simply ignored the orders. It was not clear, however, whether the Railroad Commission could legally set proration limits for the purpose of affecting the market rather than for protection of the environment. After a federal court ruled that proration limits discriminated against small operators, Gov. Ross Sterling called a special session of the legislature, which in 1933 authorized the commission to set a total volume for the East Texas field and prorated a percentage of that total production for each well. The first allotted figure was 750,000 barrels of oil daily for the field.

It's a Good Thing That We Change Governors - By Jack Patton
—Journal Staff Artist.

"It's a Good Thing That We Change Governors"
Jack Patton
January 14, 1935
Dallas Journal

Mrs. Ferguson's second administration generated less political controversy than did either her earlier term or that of her husband. Nevertheless, charges of corruption soon surfaced. Critics complained in particular of a return to her previous generosity in pardoning convicts. The critics linked that policy with the governor's dismissal of forty-four Rangers, whom she replaced with men of dubious character. The governor in addition issued "Special Ranger" commissions to almost twenty-five hundred men, thus using the force as a form of political patronage. These criticisms blended with others, and Mrs. Ferguson announced in 1934 that she intended to follow the two-term tradition and not seek re-election. In this image Jack Patton celebrates the decision of Mrs. Ferguson not to run again and laments what the cartoonist identifies as the collapse of the Texas prison system during the Ferguson administration.

"Thou Shalt Not Bear False Witness"
Cartoonist unknown
July, 1936
Plain Dealer

The Great Depression dominated politics in the elections of 1934 and 1936, as the older issues of Fergusonism and Prohibition disappeared. Seven men announced for the post of governor, but James V. Allred of Wichita Falls, the attorney general (1931–35), soon emerged as the front-runner in 1934. His major opponent was Tom F. Hunter, also of Wichita Falls, who forced Allred into a runoff in 1934. Allred won the second primary by about 40,000 votes and Hunter challenged him again in 1936. Despite his outspoken conservatism, Allred was identified closely with the New Deal and Roosevelt. Although critics charged the governor with not being sympathetic enough toward the poor, most campaigners chose to run on personality rather than challenge Allred's perceived New Deal stance. Consequently, the 1936 campaign was often one of character assassination rather than substance. Allred won the Democratic primary in 1936 without a runoff.

"Texas Rookie Goes Up"
Jack Patton
April 30, 1937
Dallas Journal

After working for the successful candidacy of Richard Kleberg in the 1931 congressional race for Texas' 14th District, Lyndon Baines Johnson went to Washington as the new congressman's legislative aide. The young Johnson won a reputation for his legislative expertise and in 1935 moved back to Texas to become the youngest state director of the National Youth Administration, a New Deal agency designed to employ needy public school and college students. The twenty-six-year-old administrator received praise both locally and nationally for his fairness and effectiveness. After Congressman James Paul Buchanan of the 10th Congressional District died in 1937, Johnson defeated eight opponents in a special election. Johnson ran as an avid supporter of the Roosevelt administration, including endorsing the president's controversial Supreme Court packing plan. As this post-election cartoon shows, he went to Washington pledging to support the New Deal.

"Ain't We Got No Rights No More?" . . . —By Kno

"Ain't We Got No Rights No More?"
John Knott
December 10, 1937
Dallas Morning News

Laws requiring registration of firearms have long been a source of controversy in Texas. In 1937 Andrew Patton, the district attorney for Dallas, and other Texans proposed that the legislature consider a law mandating registration of handguns. The stance of this cartoon was that the time had not come when carrying a gun was no longer an accepted right. The bill failed.

"Where the Lynching Is Needed"
M. A. Dunning
January 24, 1939
Austin American-Statesman

By 1936, many members of the Texas establishment were disenchanted with the New Deal. Roosevelt's popularity with the average voter discouraged most Texas leaders from distancing themselves from the program that year. Roosevelt's attack on the Supreme Court in 1937, followed by the pro-union Wagner Act, allowed many conservatives to attack the New Deal on grounds of its centralization of power. Among the pieces of legislation conservatives criticized was a federal anti-lynching bill, which threatened traditional southern race relations. It passed the House in late 1937, but a Senate filibuster, led by Texas senator Tom Connally, killed it. It was reintroduced in 1939; the cartoonist urges here that once more the bill be defeated.

"Monkey on His Back"
Jack Patton
Circa 1939
Dallas Journal

W. Lee "Pappy" O'Daniel, a flour merchant and Texas folk hero, won the gubernatorial election of 1938 with a plank that included the abolition of the poll tax (which he had not paid, preventing him from voting), opposition to capital punishment, state assistance for all elderly, and a promise of no sales tax. His first term of office (1939–41) broke into an open warfare with the legislature. His campaign promise of aid to all elderly changed to a guarantee of at least thirty dollars a month for needy older citizens. Even though a majority of the legislature supported the idea, it failed for lack of appropriations. O'Daniel proposed a transaction tax to be levied to pay for the pension plan. Opponents pointed out that his plan was a thinly disguised sales tax. The 46th Legislature closed with no tax bill and a state deficit.

"It Was a Bad Accident"
Jack Patton
August 15, 1939
Dallas Journal

The issue of oil pumped and refined in excess of legal limits did not end with the Sterling administration. "Hot oil" continued to be produced in East Texas throughout the mid-thirties. Ernest O. Thompson became chairman of the Railroad Commission and devoted himself to establishing order and proration in the East Texas field. In 1935, the Connally Act (named for Sen. Tom Connally of Texas) made it illegal to send hot oil across state lines. The combination of state and federal regulations allowed the Texas Railroad Commission to effectively set the price of oil by controlling production. When the price per barrel dropped too low, as it did in 1939, the commission would restrict production until the price rose. The discovery of the Arabian fields eliminated any power the state might have had over establishing an international price for oil.

"I Will Accept the Nomination"
Hal Coffman
December 19, 1939
Fort Worth Star-Telegram

Franklin Delano Roosevelt's second term was drawing to a close, and most observers could not imagine that he would break the two-term precedent and run a third time. John Nance Garner made a brief announcement in Uvalde, Texas, that he would accept the nomination if the delegates chose him. Vice-President Garner took the position that the office should seek the man and indicated that he would accept the nomination if offered but would not actively campaign for it. Of course, Roosevelt decided to break with tradition, and Garner, who had developed well-known differences with the president, wound up with no presidential nomination and out of the vice-presidency as well.

The Fightin' Forties (1940–49)

Political cartooning was jolted in lasting ways by our sudden entry into World War II after Pearl Harbor. Certainly through the 1930s there were cartoons about the international situation—either warning of the dangers of entanglement or arguing for intervention—although the vast majority of cartoons focused on local and national concerns like the depression, economics, and politics.

But when the debate over foreign policy shifted abruptly to rallies for morale and victory, Texas cartoonists found that the momentous subjects were actually local issues. Defense plants cropped up across the Lone Star State, and oil and agriculture took on added importance.

Several Texas cartoonists typified life in America during turbulent times: the famed John Knott cartooned throughout World War I, the Great Depression, and finally World War II; so, in his quiet way, did Houston institution Sidney Van Ulm. The modest "Van"—who was also a sports columnist, specializing in golf—was a staple of the old *Houston Press*, a favorite of readers and editorial staff alike. His style was somewhat minimalist, and he drew almost exclusively on local subjects—except during World War II and the Korean War.

Ferman Martin joined the *Houston Chronicle* in 1937 as the punchline to what became a famous story of persistence. Turned down for a cartooning job, Martin began mailing semiweekly cartoons to the editor for months picturing his own plight as a job-seeker. Finally, Martin pictured himself circling a windowless *Chronicle* building with the caption "still looking for an opening." Shortly afterwards, Martin received a wire that read, "Come on down. We've had enough." In the 1940s Martin's unique style brought sometimes pungent, sometimes wry comment on the war, picturing Hitler as a madman. Following Knott's footsteps, Martin also developed the familar character Mr. Texas, who after the war saw the state grow to unparalleled prosperity, with all the difficult problems growth brings.

While John Knott was continuing to distinguish himself as an institution, another cartoonist emerged from down the road at the *Tyler Courier Times*. Sam Nash had joined the paper in 1936 to draw cartoons and operate electronic engraving machines. He left to go into the service during World War II, then resumed his editorial cartooning at the paper after the war. It was then that he produced his "only child": a slightly rotund, balding, bespectacled character, Old Man Tyler, who would make occasional appearances when his creator wanted to speak his mind. Though he was overshadowed by many cartoonists from the big city, Nash became a small-town institution and has continued drawing at the Tyler paper for more than half a century.

Another bridger of issues and eras was Jack Howells Ficklen (nicknamed "Herc," short for Hercules, in honor of his prowess at destroying sand castles as a boy), who drew for the *Dallas Morning News*. Although he joined the paper in 1928 as a copyboy and became its sports cartoonist in 1937, it was as a substitute for the vacationing John Knott that Ficklen gained acceptance as a political cartoonist before World War II. Then the war played a role in his career: Ficklen left the *News* to serve in the army and achieved the rank of lieutenant colonel; but even when in uniform he cartooned. Ficklen drew one of the war's most beloved strips, "You're in the Army Now." Ficklen was a fixture on the Dallas scene until retirement in 1976, by which time he had helped launch the career of Austin's Ben Sargent.

On the other side of the ideological spectrum, after the war, was the liberal descendant of the *Rolling Stone* magazine of the 1800s: the *Texas Spectator*, founded in Austin by three newspapermen in 1945. A cartoonist for this paper who later distinguished himself in another field was attorney Robert C. Eckhardt. The artist, who originally signed his work "Jack O'Diamonds" because his government job forced him to use a pseudonym, later represented Houston in the U.S. House of Representatives. The Jack O'Diamonds editorial cartoon graced the entire front page of most of the issues of the *Spectator* before the paper died in 1948, its final editorial and cartoon denying charges of being "red" and of accepting funds from radical unions.

And so, unknowingly, the *Spectator* provided another "bridge"—to an overriding issue of the following decade in Texas and across the nation.

"Heave Ho"
John Knott
January 25, 1940
Dallas Morning News

The issue of civil service reform and political appointees dates at least as far back as Andrew Jackson. The assumption that the political victors have the right to award the spoils of public office to their supporters came under attack again during the Great Depression. The issue flared up particularly in January, 1940, when some state employees of the prison system were fired. As the cartoonist points out here, the legislature has never welcomed civil service reform. Proponents argue that merit testing would preserve experience in government and save taxpayer dollars. In 1947 a merit system was applied to police and fire departments in cities of over one hundred thousand population. That act has been bracketed and amended to include other professions and urban areas. Federal regulations, particularly under civil rights legislation, have included job-protection provisions for other public employees. But there still exists no open competition through merit testing for state civil service appointments.

"His Favorite Recipe"
Jack Patton
April 15, 1940
W. Lee O'Daniel News

W. Lee "Pappy" O'Daniel announced on his radio show in 1938 that he intended to run for governor on the platform of the Ten Commandments and the Golden Rule. The other twelve candidates refused to take the flour salesman seriously. "Pappy" O'Daniel was a shrewd politician, and he knew how to use radio and tent shows to capture the support of the rural poor. He won in 1938 without a runoff, and his first term was marked by bitter warfare with the legislature. He ran for re-election in 1940 advocating a transaction tax—a euphemism for a state sales tax. O'Daniel's key radio-show slogan was "Pass the biscuits, Pappy." Here, he uses his own newspaper to trumpet the tax cause and to remind the voters of his entertainment notoriety. Although he was re-elected that year, the tax did not pass the legislature.

"That's a Good Idea!" . . . . . . —By Don Grant

"That's a Good Idea!"
Don Grant
March 16, 1941
Dallas Morning News

Possibly Governor O'Daniel's only deeply held political conviction was an antipathy towards labor unions. His animosity played no part in the 1938 or 1940 political campaigns. But after re-election, facing a stalemate once more with the legislature, the governor advocated a state law that would protect defense industries against strikes. He called a special session of the legislature in 1941, which passed legislation that outlawed violence or the threat of violence to prevent anyone from working. The intent was to prevent picketers from stopping strike breakers entering into shut-down plants. It seemed unlikely that organized labor—15 percent of the industrial workforce in Texas—was any real threat to domestic order. Nevertheless, the act was popular with conservatives and gave O'Daniel a new political slogan: "corrupt labor bosses" replaced "professional politicians" as his chief whipping boys. Note fill-in cartoonist Don Grant's use of John Knott's stalwart "Old Man Texas" character.

"Out After the Big One"
Jack Patton
May 7, 1942
Dallas Journal

Governor O'Daniel's political life took a new turn in 1941, when Sen. Morris Sheppard, a supporter of the New Deal, died in office. The governor appointed eighty-seven-year-old Andrew Jackson Houston, the infirm son of Sam Houston, as U.S. senator. "Pappy" then made his plans to run in the special election for the Senate. Twenty-eight other candidates announced for the election, including the young congressman Lyndon B. Johnson. Johnson and O'Daniel led in the first primary and entered the runoff. In a very close election, the governor defeated the congressman by slightly more than one thousand votes. Many of these votes trickled in late from East Texas precincts, where O'Daniel had the support of the poor and the elderly. Johnson always believed that illicit votes cost him the election. O'Daniel won a regular term in 1942, when he defeated James Allred in the race for the Senate.

"No Mexican Served"
Cartoonist unknown
Circa 1944

In many parts of Texas, Hispanics faced the same type of segregation as did blacks. This amateur cartoon dramatizes the attitude of Mexican Americans. In Texas, civil rights organizations began to demand in the 1940s that segregation end. Led by the League of United Latin American Citizens and, after the Second World War, G.I. Forum, Hispanic organizations began to sue in federal courts to end segregation. In a landmark case, *Delgado* v. *Bastrop Independent School District* (1948), Mexican-American lawyers convinced a federal court that classroom segregation violated the Fourteenth Amendment. In 1954 the U.S. Supreme Court ruled that qualified Mexican Americans could not be excluded from juries. Such cases eroded discriminatory customs common south of San Antonio.

"Back Door Cabinet Lockout Looming"
Cartoonist unknown
September 26, 1944
W. Lee O'Daniel News

W. Lee O'Daniel billed himself as an anti–New Deal senator. In 1944 he spearheaded the Texas Regulars campaign, which endorsed no presidential candidate but offered a slate of uncommitted electors to the voters. In this cartoon from his promotional newspaper, O'Daniel identifies the back door of the White House as a place where labor unions, African Americans, big-city bosses and corrupt politicians, and Communists come to seek favors. The implicit promise of the Texas Regulars was that such activities would end when Roosevelt was defeated and white supremacy was restored. Roosevelt garnered 821,000 votes in Texas to Republican nominee Thomas Dewey's 191,000 and the Regulars' 135,000. The division within the Democratic party did not heal, however.

"The Last Drop"
Ferman Martin
Circa 1945
Houston Chronicle

Texans, like most other Americans, enthusiastically supported the Second World War. As Hitler's defeat became only a matter of time, the war ended up being more than a patriotic venture for Texas. Blessed with a good climate and powerful congressmen, the state attracted a sizable national investment in military bases. In addition, a long coastline, an abundance of oil, and the political clout to acquire defense contracts enhanced a booming defense industry. The Cold War developing after 1945 encouraged a standing army and increased defense spending. Texas benefited accordingly. World War II thus had begun the industrialization and urbanization of modern Texas. The state population, which was 55 percent rural in 1940, was 63 percent urban when the 1950 census was taken.

PRODIGAL'S RETURN?

"Prodigal's Return?"
Bill Saylor
March 22, 1946
Texas Spectator

W. Lee O'Daniel decided by 1945 that he could not win re-election to the Senate in 1948. The state had become too urban, many of his advisors said, to support his candidacy. Nor had he been a particularly effective senator. Political rumors surfaced that O'Daniel intended to resign from the Senate in 1946 and announce as a conservative candidate for the Democratic gubernatorial nomination. This cartoon—from the liberal journal the *Texas Spectator*—shows "Pappy" returning from Washington, D.C., to run for governor with the enthusiastic endorsement of rural Texans. O'Daniel decided not to make the race. He did run for governor in 1956 on a profoundly racist platform, placing third behind Price Daniel and Ralph Yarborough. He did, however, garner more than 300,000 votes in that race, with his strength remaining in East Texas.

THE VETERAN'S FRIENDS

"The Veteran's Friends"
Jack O'Diamonds
November 1, 1946
Texas Spectator

Just after the war, Texas Land Commissioner Bascom Giles proposed a constitutional amendment to authorize state-guaranteed loans enabling veterans to purchase land cheaply. The amendment passed, and the state began to buy land for resale to veterans. Some publications warned early on that the scheme had a potential for scandal. From its inception rumors developed that the veteran's land board was tricking unwary veterans into selling their right for land purchase to speculators and that the land commissioner was accepting bribes for special favors in granting loans and evaluating land prices. This cartoon was drawn by "Jack O'Diamonds"—as indicated by the symbol of the figure in the stall in the lower left corner—a Houston attorney who later became known as Congressman Bob Eckhardt.

"South"
Cartoonist unknown
January 25, 1947
Dallas Express

World War II increased demands that African Americans receive social justice at home. Hitler's assertion of the inferiority of non-Germanic humanity gave racism a bad name. In addition, the migration of black people to the North created voting blocs that could determine elections. By 1947, there appeared a goodly number of black and white Americans who campaigned for an end to Jim Crow legislation in the South.

"Bracero"
Herc Ficklen
Circa 1947
Dallas Morning News

During the Great Depression, there were several "roundups" to send
undocumented workers back to Mexico. The shortage of labor during
the war, however, persuaded the United States to create a *bracero*
program, which permitted temporary workers to come from Mexico
and harvest crops. Pressure from large growers continued the program
after the war. Both Mexico and the United States complained of abuses
in the program. The migrant workers were not always adequately
cared for as prescribed by law, and many of the migrants used the entry
visas as opportunities to settle in large urban barrios. In 1967, the
program was suspended, but the issues of illegal immigration and
mistreatment of farm workers persisted.

THE 80 - YEAR SLEEP

"The 80-Year Sleep"
Jack O'Diamonds
March 28, 1948
Texas Spectator

Some politicians in southern states and their supporters decided to mount a third-party challenge to Democratic president Harry S Truman in 1948. Labeling themselves Dixiecrats, the third party charged the president with betraying the South by endorsing civil rights and integrating the armed services by executive order. The Dixiecrats had little hope of success, but it was possible that the party might drain off enough Democratic voters to elect Republican Thomas E. Dewey president. This cartoon depicts the Dixiecrats as awakening from a pre-Reconstruction slumber and wishing to turn back the clock to 1868. The Dixiecrats nominated Strom Thurmond, a Democratic senator from South Carolina, for the presidency. Truman carried Texas by over a million votes—the most lopsided victory in the nation. Thurmond won less than 7 percent of the Texas ballots.

"Coke Stevenson"
Herc Ficklen
Circa 1948
Dallas Morning News

Lt. Gov. Coke Stevenson succeeded O'Daniel as governor in 1941 and was re-elected in 1942 and 1944. In 1948 Stevenson ran for the U.S. Senate and was challenged by Lyndon Johnson, who still chafed from the controversial defeat in the 1941 special election. The campaign was bitterly fought, with most liberals supporting Johnson. Stevenson led in the first primary but lost in the second by eighty-seven votes. The ex-governor charged that Johnson stole the election, and charges of voter fraud surfaced from both camps. After a contentious Democratic state executive committee meeting that upheld Johnson's nomination and a court order that placed him on the general ballot, Johnson went on to win the senatorial seat. The charge of a corrupt election haunted LBJ until his death. Conservatives in particular argued that the campaign of 1948 betrayed Stevenson. In this image, for example, the cartoonist draws Stevenson as a rock of integrity.

Embarrassing, Isn't It?

"Embarrassing, Isn't It?"
Sam Nash
June 7, 1949
Tyler Courier Times

Gov. Beauford Jester had won the gubernatorial election of 1946 with Allan Shivers as his lieutenant governor. Together, they represented the "Texas Establishment." They campaigned on the issues of no new taxes, no federal interference with state laws, and opposition to labor unions. At the same time they campaigned for reform of public schools and higher appropriations for roads, prisons, colleges, and charitable institutions, especially state hospitals for the insane. However, the legislature barely had enough money to pay for all the items it had made appropriations for, much less new public buildings. When Governor Jester died in office in 1949, Shivers took over the gubernatorial duties and addressed a special session of the legislature. Using such phrases as "Texas ranks first in goats but last in care for the wards of the state," and "first in oil but last in mental hospitals," the governor called upon the legislature to accept more responsibility for the unfortunate. Appropriations for the needy did increase, but the state continued to rank near the bottom in social services, claiming no money and no new taxes.

The Fearful Fifties (1950–59)

Unlike the aftermath of World War I, the post-WWII period of the late 1940s had demonstrated that America could not avoid a prominent role in international affairs; its only choice was whether to play the role well or poorly. Fueled by this imperative—which was heated in particular by a sudden expansionism on the part of the Soviet Union and mingled legitimate and hysterical fears of Communist infiltration in the United States—Texas cartooning activity took on an increasingly heated tone in the 1950s.

With the spread of television, newspapers and magazines found themselves obliged to seek aggressive new ways of competing for attention. Encouraged by the increasing complexity of issues, the print media deepened their analytical approach and offered more informative products. They found an ideal vehicle in cartooning. A heightened emphasis nationwide on cartoon commentary brought increased exposure for Texas 'toonmeisters in major Eastern newspapers as well as the likes of *Time* and *Newsweek*.

Established artists kept busy, and newcomer Bill McClanahan hit the ground running with the new decade. Embodying an aggressive conservatism suited to Texas' emerging Republican voice, McClanahan actually had joined the *Dallas Morning News* during the 1930s but experienced a false start, his career—like that of Herc Ficklen—having been interrupted by the war. McClanahan resumed his climb to prominence in 1946; he broke through a little later than Ficklen, and after 1957, when John Knott retired, the two shared political-'toon duties on the *News*. McClanahan voiced his philosophy: "An editorial cartoon should attack, not boost." He confined his boosterism to the realm of sports, in which he pursued virtually a parallel career, designing program covers for the Cotton Bowl and the Dallas Cowboys, creating mascot characters for Southwest Conference teams, and painting portraits for the University of Arkansas Sports Hall of Fame. McClanahan retired in 1972 and died in 1981.

A gentler approach—although no less thoroughly Texan—was represented by Harold Maples, who joined the *Fort Worth Star-Telegram* in 1954 after stints with the *Scurry County Times*, the *Abilene Reporter-News*, and the *Snyder Daily News*. His samples were endorsed by the retiring legend of the *Star-Telegram*, Hal Coffman, in this succinct appraisal: "He's got it!" Drawing in a playful style that reflected the influence of Herblock and Vaughn Shoemaker, Maples became a Fort Worth institution during his nearly thirty years with the *Star-Telegram*.

"Back to Work"
Herc Ficklen
1952
Dallas Morning News

Martin Dies, from Orange, won election to Congress in 1931 as the House's youngest member. In 1938 he became chair of the newly created House Un-American Activities Committee (HUAC, usually identified as the Dies Committee). The committee investigated Nazi activities but became better known for its activities in searching out those Dies identified as subversive: labor unions, New Deal sympathizers, and alleged Communists. Dies retired because of ill health in 1945, the same year that HUAC was made a permanent House committee, but he returned to Congress in 1952. This cartoon celebrates his victory in an at-large election and his return to HUAC. The congressman lost in special elections for the U.S. Senate in 1941 and 1957. He served out the remainder of his term in Congress after the last loss, then retired.

"Eisenhower Delegates"
Hal Coffman
1952
Fort Worth Star-Telegram

The Republican party was divided in 1950 between the Old Guard, who supported Robert Taft, the conservative senator from Ohio, and the moderate Republicans, who endorsed Dwight David Eisenhower. The division was reflected in Texas, where Eisenhower's popularity had attracted a number of conservative Democrats. In urban areas, some of these potential Republican voters attended precinct conventions and elected delegates to attend the state convention pledged to support Eisenhower's nomination. The Old Guard charged that these new recruits were not really Republicans and wanted to steal the nomination from Taft. The Republican split in Texas received national publicity, especially when two Texas delegations went to the 1952 Republican convention, dramatically illustrating fights within the party. Eventually at Chicago the moderate wing prevailed, and Eisenhower was nominated.

"The Thundering Herd"
Ferman Martin
1952
Houston Chronicle

The Texas election law was changed in 1951 so that candidates could cross-file, or run as both a Democratic and a Republican nominee. Conservative cross-filing in Texas was encouraged by the Democratic party's national stand that the tidelands or adjacent underwater oil lands belonged to the federal government. "Ike" Republicans supported cross-filing, hoping that conservative Democrats would endorse Dwight D. Eisenhower's election to the presidency and eventually defect to the Republican party. Taft forces argued that cross-filing would limit the growth of state parties. The ideological battle continued at the state convention in Mineral Wells and the national convention in Chicago. Ike won the nomination, endorsed returning tidelands to the states, and defeated Adlai Stevenson for the presidency. Texas voted for Ike, and most statewide Democratic candidates cross-filed.

FINANCE LESSON

"Finance Lesson"
Herc Ficklen
February 11, 1953
Dallas Morning News

The state legislature passed the three Gilmer-Aiken laws in 1949, reorganizing the Texas public school system and establishing a formula for minimum teachers' salaries that included shared funding between state and local governments. Although these reforms were long overdue, critics quickly pointed out inadequacies. The funding relied on consumer taxes, and without stable appropriations, inadequate financing would always haunt education. Moreover, the salaries of teachers were woefully low, and the need for compensation that would keep abreast of the cost of living surfaced as a political issue again in 1953. Texas teacher salaries have rarely matched the national average, and this disparity continues to be a contentious issue. In addition, the funding of a public school system by minimum state monies matched with some local funds became equally controversial.

By BOB TAYLOR, Times Herald Staff Cartoonist

—AND BUOYS WILL BE BUOYS

"And Buoys Will Be Buoys"
Bob Taylor
1954
Dallas Times Herald

The Submerged Lands Act of 1954 gave states the "historic bound-aries" of their coastal lands. Immediately, quarrels arose among various states and the federal government over where the historic boundaries should be drawn. Texas claimed 10½ miles, based on the boundaries of the Republic rather than the traditional three miles as cited by practice in international law. Louisiana did likewise, and a federal suit against that state eventually drew the other Gulf Coast states into litigation. The U.S. Supreme Court ruled in 1960 that Texas' historic boundaries did extend to their claimed limit, but that those of Louisiana, Missis-sippi, and Alabama did not. This suit ended a thirteen-year controversy in which cartoonists drew hundreds of cartoons about the issue, includ-ing this representative one, by Bob Taylor.

"A CIVIL RIGHTS LAW WILL HELP TAKE THE PROFIT OUT OF SEGREGATION."

"A Civil Rights Law Will Help . . . "
Cartoonist unknown
April 3, 1954
Houston Informer

By the spring of 1954, African-American newspapers were celebrating the *Brown* v. *Board* of Education decision, which declared segregation of public schools illegal. They were also urging the federal government and their allies to attack segregation elsewhere in society. The *Houston Informer*, one of a chain of African-American newspapers owned by Carter Wesley, a Houston lawyer and publisher, demanded passage of a civil rights act, which would void other Jim Crow legislation. Here the *Informer* derides real estate entrepreneurs whom it accuses of exploiting restrictive real estate covenants to force black Americans to pay high costs for inferior, segregated housing rather than buying residences on the open market. The *Informer* suggests that special interests were willing to combine with white southerners to defeat civil rights acts and to protect segregation in order to economically exploit a minority population.

"Down to the Wire"
Sidney Van Ulm
November, 1954
Houston Press

Gov. Allan Shivers ran for an unprecedented third term in 1954. The gubernatorial campaign was one of the more vitriolic in Texas history. The governor had endorsed Dwight David Eisenhower in the 1952 presidential campaign. His opponent, Ralph Yarborough—who had lost to Shivers in 1952—attacked the governor's stand, arguing that "Shivercrats" were really closet Republicans. Moreover, Yarborough tried to link the governor with a mounting scandal in the insurance business. Shivers, in turn, charged that Yarborough was unduly influenced by labor unions—which were controlled, according to the governor, by the Communists. As the cartoon implies, the race went down to the wire, with Shivers winning a narrow re-election victory.

"Candidate for Boot Hill"
Harold Maples
March 6, 1955
Fort Worth Star-Telegram

Controversy over the Texas Rangers in politics has appeared with some regularity throughout Texas history. Homer Garrison, head of the Department of Public Safety, modernized the Rangers in the 1940s by increasing their familiarity with technology and expanding their numbers. Nevertheless, critics continued to charge that the Rangers were not and had never been sympathetic to minorities. Indeed, the organization was charged with persecuting Hispanic citizens south of San Antonio. Critics also maintained that the Rangers were anti-union and served as strikebreakers. A bill in 1955 would have abolished the Rangers, but it did not pass. Controversy did not cease, but rather increased in the 1960s, particularly as the organization became widely perceived as anti-Mexican. The Department of Public Safety reorganized the Rangers in 1974, with an accent on training, technology, and recruitment of minorities. Nevertheless, as late as the 1980s, civil rights groups still charged that the Rangers did not actively recruit minority officers.

"Smellier by the Day"
Harold Maples
March 7, 1955
Fort Worth Star-Telegram

The Land Board, composed of the governor, the land commissioner, and the attorney general, approved of the loans and of the applications from veterans for the purchase of lands with state-guaranteed loans at low interest rates. In 1954 the *Cuero Record* investigated rumors that Bascom Giles was inflating land values and using other fraudulent tactics to embezzle funds. At first, big-city dailies paid little attention to the charges, but by 1955 rumors persisted that the Land Board was rife with corruption, and the media began to demand an investigation of the agency. The veterans' land scandal became a major issue in Gov. Allan Shivers's second administration, since he had served on the Land Board. Giles later confessed to criminal charges, including accepting bribes from land speculators, and was sent to prison.

"Insurance"
Bill McClanahan
January 4, 1956
Dallas Morning News

In December, 1955, the U.S. Trust & Guaranty Insurance Company failed. The company was based in Texas, but controlled seventy-four insurance companies in twenty-two other states. Indeed, Texas' insurance laws were so lax that more companies operated in this state than in all others combined. A legislative investigation criticized the State Board of Insurance for accepting gifts from Ben Jack Cage, who had founded the ICT Insurance Company, which had also gone bankrupt. Cage was indicted for embezzlement, but he fled to Brazil. Gov. Price Daniel in 1957 appointed an investigative commission to further scrutinize insurance operations. The body proposed sixteen new regulatory laws. Most of these did not pass in their original form, and insurance regulation remained an issue.

"Twice in the Same Place"
Ferman Martin
Circa 1956
Houston Chronicle

Allan Shivers led the conservative Democratic bolt in 1952 that endorsed the Republican Eisenhower for the presidency. All of the state officials except John White, the commissioner of agriculture, cross-listed as both Democratic and Republican candidates. Ike won the state with 53 percent of the vote, and the Democrats for Eisenhower organization raised a considerable amount of money. The organization included such well-known Texans as Ted Dealy of the *Dallas Morning News*, Jesse Jones and William P. Hobby of Houston, and Amon Carter of the *Fort Worth Star-Telegram*. The organization was almost a Who's Who of Texas Democrats. In 1956, however, the support for Ike lacked enthusiasm. Stevenson was considered by most observers a cinch loser. Even though the cartoon shows Shivers's bolt striking Stevenson twice, the cross-filing of conservative Democrats for office in 1956 had little effect on the outcome. The president won an easy victory.

Betwixt and Between

"Betwixt and Between"
Harold Maples
March 30, 1956
Fort Worth Star-Telegram

The 1956 Democratic party division created serious problems for Lyndon B. Johnson. The senator had aspirations for national office by this time, and he wanted to lead the state Democratic delegation to the national convention and receive the state's nominating ballots as a favorite son for the presidency. If he led the Texas delegation, he would have to compromise with Shivers's supporters and still retain the support from the labor-liberal wing of the party. LBJ finally wrested control of the convention away from the Shivers forces and received the support of loyalist Democrats with the promise that he would support them for positions in the state party apparatus after the 1956 election. The promises were not fulfilled, and some liberal Texas Democrats mistrusted Johnson up until his presidency.

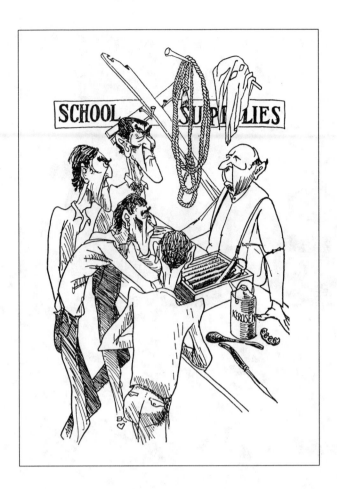

"School Supplies"
Bob Eckhardt
September 12, 1956
Texas Observer

Mansfield, a small town southeast of Fort Worth, maintained a dual school system that had no high school for black residents. They had to be bused to Fort Worth if they were to attend high school. Consequently, the Mansfield public school system was the first in the state ordered by the courts to integrate. The school board agreed in 1956, but a mob of three hundred to four hundred protesters ringed the school that fall and intercepted anyone suspected of being sympathetic to integration. The mob roughed up reporters and bystanders and threatened the sheriff and any black families who sent their children to the white schools. Gov. Allan Shivers described the mob as an orderly protest and sent in the Texas Rangers to support them, preventing integration. In this cartoon, the mob is seen buying supplies to begin the school term.

"Hem, Haw, Hope"
Hal Coffman
Circa 1957
Fort Worth Star-Telegram

Until World War II, water usage and control had little importance to Texans, except for arguments over surface rights. But the bitter drought of the 1950s forced the state government to consider some plan for water management. Governor Shivers created the Water Pollution Control Board and the Texas Water Research Committee to investigate water usage. Neither of those two boards or the legislature did much except to "hem, haw, and hope" that the problem would solve itself. The state in 1957 allotted money to local agencies for use by water resources. Localism, regionalism, and the Corp of Engineers took control, and coordinated planning for water has yet to come to the state.

BY BOB TAYLOR,
Staff Cartoonist

GETTING NOWHERE IN A BIG HURRY

"Getting Nowhere in a Big Hurry"
Bob Taylor
Circa 1958
Dallas Times Herald

This 1958 image suggests some of the political problems that conservative Democratic politicians and voters faced in Texas. Spurred on by the 1957 Civil Rights Act and growing crises over desegregation of the public schools in Little Rock and elsewhere, conservatives accused both Republican President Dwight David Eisenhower and the northern Democratic party of being too supportive of an active central government. These critics suggested that politicians needed to return to states' rights and limited government. But as this image suggests such a political stance placed progress in a holding pattern. Those same voters who wished to limit the power of the federal government were unwilling to raise state taxes to provide for responsible state services or economic growth.

"Hope of a Two Party State"
Hal Coffman
1959
Fort Worth Star-Telegram

Although Eisenhower's presidential victories in Texas were significant, the president did not have very long coattails. Republicans did not win many local, state, or national elections. Many observers thought that a two-party state would offer the voters more real choices. Here Texas is viewing the frail condition of the Republican party and hoping that the party survives to mount challenges to the Democratic establishment. Historians disagree upon when the real birth of the two-party state began. Some suggest that in the 1950s Republican organizations in the suburbs laid a grass-roots network that built a foundation for future successes. Eisenhower support spurred on these organizations. Others argue that the election of John Tower to the U.S. Senate in 1961 gave the party visibility that began its real challenge to Democratic control of the state.

The Assertion of Conservatism (1960–69)

On November 22, 1963, the nation was stunned by the news of Pres. John F. Kennedy's assassination in Dallas, Texas. In what some people thought was a cartoonist's premonition, Herc Ficklen's cartoon that morning had Kennedy and Lyndon Johnson riding in a jeep bouncing over the Texas Hill Country. The image had Kennedy with a rifle that was similiar to the one that shot him later that day, taking aim at a deer labeled Texas' twenty-four electoral votes. Texas would from then on be known as the state in which our thirty-fifth president was murdered.

Kennedy came to the state because its traditional conservatism took a further swing to the right in the 1960s. The Republican party gained significant footholds in local and statewide elections, and the results were felt beyond state borders, as the Democratic party's "Solid South" coalition began to crumble. Political careers were made or broken in the light of the civil rights movement and the growing conflict in Vietnam.

The intensification of right-wing sentiments made Lyndon Baines Johnson—a New-Deal Democrat and a favorite son out of favor with conservative elements—an unlikely Texas politician to assume the presidency of the United States. But the assassination of John F. Kennedy, ironically in Texas, did result in LBJ's accession.

Johnson loomed large on the national horizon during his presidency (1963–69). He initiated and supported a variety of liberal social programs while escalating a war that was opposed by liberal elements. Eventually LBJ himself became the issue; he retired from the race in 1968, only to see his vice-president, Hubert H. Humphrey, lose to a resurrected Richard M. Nixon in the general election.

The decade ended in extreme turbulence—with war protests inspiring a social revolution; George Wallace attracting disaffected voters to a conservative platform; and the assassination of several more political leaders, including Martin Luther King, Jr., and Bobby Kennedy.

In addition to the death of John Kennedy, the cartoon-loving public would feel the loss of the creater of Old Man Texas, John Knott. His death in February, 1963, came after a lengthy illness which prevented him from practicing his craft. He had once explained his profession by commenting that "every child at some period of life has the imitative instinct and wants to draw. Some of them grow up and get over it. They become normal people. The others turn into artists."

Observers might note that the rest of Texas' corps of cartoonist-commentators were subdued in their observations of the events of the sixties, even when it came to another local-cum-national issue, the bribery scandal involving LBJ aide Bille Sol Estes. Perhaps the artists felt themselves to be the thoughtful eyes in the center of the hurricane. Another factor might be that the 1960s represented the changing of the guard—the ends of careers for cartoonists of traditional tone, commentators whose gentility outweighed vitriol. But the times, they were a-changin'.

Tom Darcy, who joined the *Houston Post* in 1964, was one of the earliest cartoonists in the country to draw cartoons that opposed the Vietnam War. His incisive cartoons on the war and his hard-hitting and poignant commentaries on racial discrimination and the plight of the poor eventually led to his dismissal from the *Post* in 1966 and a Pulitzer Prize in 1970 while cartooning for *Newsday*.

Other cartoonists in Texas were making names for themselves. Bob Taylor, having joined the *Dallas Times Herald* in 1958, created well-drawn, free-wheeling, memorable cartoons. C. P. Houston went to the *Houston Chronicle* for advice on how to become a cartoonist and ended up being hired as their editorial cartoonist in 1965, following Ferman Martin's retirement. Bill Saylor continued to stick needles into the impervious hide of the Texas legislature. Saylor was a cartoonist who commanded many styles. But his true forte was a free-flowing expressionist line that models through dark and light areas. The profession also continued to be represented by Herc Ficklen and Bill McClanahan in their traditional styles and their neighbor, the gentle Harold Maples of the *Fort Worth Star-Telegram*.

"Well, Look at Us Texans"
Bill Saylor
May 30, 1961
Houston Post

John Tower received 900,000 votes in the 1960 senatorial contest against Lyndon Johnson, capitalizing on Johnson's decision to run simultaneously for re-election and for vice-president. In May, 1961, liberal Democrats split their votes in the special senatorial election, which had more than seventy contestants, and the run-off candidates were Tower and William Blakely, a conservative "interim" appointee to the U.S. Senate. Liberals therefore decided either to "go fishing" or to vote for Tower. They hoped that the election of conservative Republicans would lure conservative Democrats into that party, leaving them a more left-leaning party organization. Progressive voters, consequently, may have determined the outcome of the election that sent Tower—the first Republican senator from Texas since Reconstruction—to Washington. Tower's early showing and long-term endurance lent impetus to the newly assertive Republican party in Texas.

"Veto Threat"
Herc Ficklen
June 30, 1961
Dallas Morning News

Price Daniel became governor in 1956 and won again in 1958 and 1960. Many of Daniel's problems in those second two terms came from the age-old issue of taxes. He and the legislature deadlocked over raising taxes in his first term, and the issue carried over into the beginnings of his third term. Daniel opposed a general sales tax. He wanted instead an omnibus tax bill that included sin taxes and a larger share of taxes levied on business. Here, Daniel is shown clubbing back legislative demands for a sales tax. After two special sessions in 1961, the legislature passed a limited sales tax of 1 percent which exempted certain items—food, drugs, clothing, and farm supplies, for example. Daniel refused to sign the bill, and it became a law without his signature.

"Civil Rights Issue"
Ferman Martin
1962
Houston Chronicle

Gov. Price Daniel chose to run for a fourth term in 1962. Liberals supported Don Yarbrough, no relationship to Ralph Yarborough. Other candidates included former attorney general Will Wilson and retired general Edwin Walker, who flew the American flag upside-down in front of his Dallas residence to warn of what he called the dangers of integration. The fresh face in the campaign was John Connally, President Kennedy's secretary of the Navy and a longtime friend and supporter of Lyndon Johnson. Connally's close relationship with the national administration and its endorsement of civil rights is depicted in this cartoon as fraught with danger for Connally's political future. The 1962 runoff pitted Don Yarbrough against John Connally, who won by a slim margin of 26,000 votes and went on to turn back the Republican challenge in the general election.

"Carpenter-Glenn"
Harold Maples
May 5, 1962
Fort Worth Star-Telegram

President Kennedy had promised early on to create a space program that would surpass those of any other nation and eventually send a man to the moon and beyond. He founded the National Aeronautics and Space Administration (NASA) in 1961 and located a series of space laboratories around the country, including a central organization at Houston. Col. John Glenn's orbiting of the earth in February, 1962, and other early successes galvanized the American imagination. This cartoon celebrates Glenn and fellow astronaut Scott Carpenter, whose flights had given us wings and who, with astronauts yet to come, were to chart, as Kennedy put it, the uncharted oceans of space.

"Have Fun"
Harold Maples
January 13, 1963
Fort Worth Star-Telegram

Price Daniel left office in 1962 as a moderate Democrat, listing his accomplishments as beginning long-range planning for water resources, increasing the state's building program, enhancing aid for the elderly, and allocating more money for law enforcement and charitable institutions. He was always more popular with the people than the legislature. He probably stayed in office one term too long given the last term's fierce legislative battles. He is shown here turning over the reins of government to John Connally, who is to face a "log-jam" of contentious legislative issues. Connally was not particularly successful in his first term in office. His close election and divisions within the Democratic party limited his effectiveness.

"Big Game"
Herc Ficklen
November 22, 1963
Dallas Morning News

The 1960 presidential election had been a hard-fought Democratic victory in Texas, which the Kennedy-Johnson ticket won by only a 46,000-vote margin out of 2,300,000 votes cast. The Texas Democratic party was wracked by dissension shortly after the election as political allies of Vice-President Johnson and U.S. Sen. Ralph Yarborough fought for control over the state party machinery. John Connally, a Johnson protégé, won a close and acrimonious gubernatorial election in 1962. Moreover, many conservative voters were alienated by Kennedy's stand on civil rights. Kennedy and Johnson thus decided to visit Texas to seek support for the administration and to help reunify the conservative and liberal wings of the Democratic party. This cartoon depicts Kennedy drawing a bead on the state's twenty-four electoral votes, which many observers thought vital to his 1964 re-election efforts. The unintended irony of the pointed rifle is an unsettling image. On that day in Dallas, assassin Lee Harvey Oswald used a similar weapon to murder John F. Kennedy and change the course of history.

MAIN EVENT—1964?

By HERC FICKLEN
Dallas News Staff Cartoonist

"Main Event"
Herc Ficklen
1964
Dallas Morning News

President Johnson ran for re-election in 1964. The Republicans nominated Sen. Barry Goldwater of Arizona, the darling of the party's right wing and a particular favorite of Texas Republicans. Johnson wanted to make sure that his home state rallied to his cause and that the Democratic party, marked by infighting since the 1950s, closed ranks behind his candidacy. This cartoon predicts the main event of the election to be another close race between Don Yarbrough and John Connally for governor and a serious challenge to Sen. Ralph Yarborough from Lloyd Bentsen, Jr., then a popular congressman. Johnson pressured Bentsen not to run in the name of party harmony. And Connally, who had been wounded in the Kennedy assassination, had become politically unbeatable. The "main event" turned into a shoo-in as Connally easily won, Yarborough defeated a little-known radio station owner, Gordon McLendon, in the primary and Republican George Bush in the general election, and Johnson trounced Goldwater.

TOUGH BIRD TO CARVE. 1964.

"Tough Bird to Carve"
Bill McClanahan
February 25, 1964
Dallas Morning News

Redistricting controversies are as old as the United States. Indeed, the word *gerrymander* comes from the way that Gov. Elbridge Gerry drew a legislative district in 1812 in Massachusetts to guarantee the election of a supporter. As the Republican party grew stronger in Texas, the issue of redistricting after population gains shifted from a rural-urban issue to one which included issues of party interests and eventually of fair representation of ethnic and racial minorities as well. Here, clearly, the carving-up of the political spoils of Texas was going to be a difficult task. The federal courts, for example, would order Dallas to hold single-member elections for the state senate in 1965, the statehouse in 1972, and the city council in 1975. Consequently, battles over redistricting and fair elections would soon involve all aspects of federal, state, and local elections. The 1991 redistricting efforts of the state legislature, for example, would be dealt with for the most part in the federal courts.

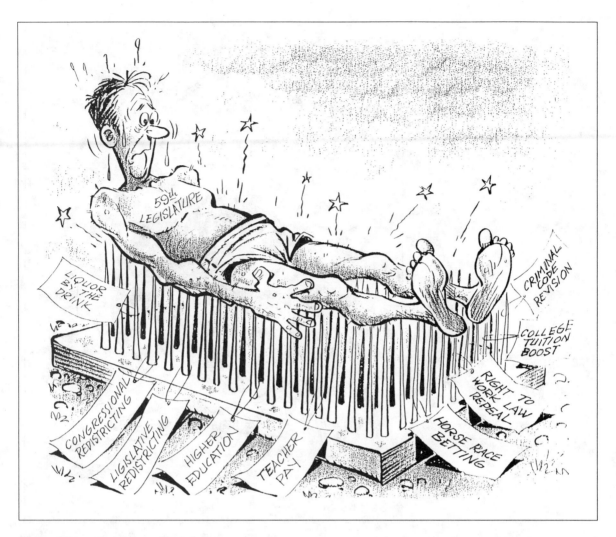

"No Bed of Roses"
Harold Maples
January 13, 1965
Fort Worth Star-Telegram

Gov. John Connally became more powerful with each succeeding election. The 1964 election also saw the emergence of Ben Barnes, a Connally supporter, as Speaker of the House. Success was hardly unqualified, however, as many of the governor's proposals were opposed by Lt. Gov. Preston Smith in the Senate. Still, the Connally-Barnes team forced the 59th Legislature to react to its "bed of nails" situation by introducing legislation that would aid public schools, revise the penal code, establish a fine arts commission, authorize liquor by the drink, raise new tax monies, reorganize health agencies and water boards, and establish a college coordinating agency. Connally was reelected in 1966 and chose to retire in 1968. Nevertheless, his political strength was such that he still led the Texas delegation to the 1968 Democratic Convention despite his announced intention not to run again.

Setting Sol

"Setting Sol"
Bob Taylor
January 21, 1965
Dallas Times Herald

Billie Sol Estes, onetime West Texas financier and friend of Lyndon Johnson, built up an empire based on fraudulent transactions, most of which were with the federal government. Oscar Giffin, reporting for the *Pecos Independent*, won a Pulitzer Prize for exposing Estes's chicanery, which involved a tangled trail of federal loans on fertilizer tanks and agricultural subsidies and cotton allotments on nonexistent or fraudulent properties. The investigation fell partially to a Senate committee led by John McClellan of Arkansas. Conservatives maintained that close connections among Vice President Johnson, Estes, and other important Democrats led McClellan to conduct only a desultory probe. Estes, who eventually declared bankruptcy, was sued for millions of dollars, given two jail terms (for eight and fifteen years), and assessed $18 million in back taxes by the IRS. Conservatives used Estes in the 1964 presidential campaign as an example of the kind of men associated with Johnson. Still, no link between the president and the financier's business dealings was ever clearly demonstrated.

"1965 Employment"
Herc Ficklen
September 2, 1965
Dallas Morning News

Although the sixties would be politically and socially tumultuous, prosperity came to Texas. The oil industry grew, and so did defense. Texas cities expanded from rather small urban centers to large metropolitan areas. Urbanization spurred construction and expansion that employed more Texans in 1965 than ever before. This cartoon celebrates both the change to an urban economy and the spread of prosperity. Issues of the environment, inner-city decay, and declining industry would wait until the next decade to rear their ugly heads.

"Lyndon Johnson"
Ben Sargent
1967
Hitherto unpublished

Even as Lyndon Johnson, in his presidency, regained the (grudging)
acceptance of the Texas liberals whom he had alienated during the 1950s,
his escalating hawkishness toward Vietnam made him a favored target
of embittered ridicule from the farther left-wing. A 1967 lyric from
songwriter Country Joe McDonald demands: "Come out, Lyndon, with
your hands held high/Drop your guns, baby, and reach for the sky."
This pencil sketch from the same period conveys a comparable attitude
with the succinct wit and compositional savvy that would propel Ben
Sargent in less than a decade to the front ranks of American editorial
cartoonists. (Note the Johnsonesque pronunciation of Vietnam at the
lower right.) Sargent was at the time a college student in the ultracon-
servative Texas Panhandle town of Amarillo, where he routinely
skewered right-wing sensibilities in a journal called the *Saddlebag*.

"Left the Gate Open"
Ferman Martin
Circa 1968
Houston Chronicle

The 1968 announcements by both Johnson and Connally that they would not run for re-election encouraged Republicans and liberal Democrats alike. Both groups were to be disappointed. Vice-President Hubert Humphrey received the Democratic nomination and ran against Richard Nixon, who represented the conservative Republicans, and George Wallace, who campaigned as an independent. Johnson and Connally rallied the Democrats behind Humphrey, whom conservatives accused of standing too close to Johnson and too staunchly in support of civil rights. Nixon, however, failed to rope the Texas longhorn, as Humphrey carried the state, but lost the national election. George Wallace garnered only 584,000 of the more than 3 million ballots cast in Texas.

"YA GOT UNTIL ELECTION DAY TO CLEAR OUT'   11/1/68 HOUSTON CHRONICLE

"Ya Got until Election Day to Clear Out"
C. P. Houston
November 1, 1968
Houston Chronicle

Liberals were disappointed in the 1968 election. The conservative
lieutenant governor Preston Smith beat the liberal Don Yarborough,
who had led the first primary, in the Democratic runoff for governor.
The Republicans chose Paul Eggers as their candidate. Eggers had the
strong support of Senator Tower and his political machine. Nevertheless, Smith defeated the challenger by winning 57 percent of the
popular vote. It was clear, then, in 1968 that conservative Democrats in
Texas could win against liberal challengers by warning conservatives of
the danger of sixties liberalism and then, in turn, by rallying minorities
and labor unions to their cause in the general election by warning of the
dangers of right-wing Republicanism. As this cartoon implies, the
Republican elephant was not yet ready to challenge the Democratic
donkey for control of the statehouse.

The Changing of the Guards (1970–79)

The nation became more divided over the Vietnam War and the civil rights movement, as civil disobedience continued on college campuses. The Vietnam War and student riots were brought into people's living rooms in ways that newspapers and editorial cartoons could never portray. The dissension in the state allowed conservative Democrats to win the primaries against many minority opponents for state legislative seats. The 1970 gubernatorial election saw the conservative Preston Smith become the first Texas Democrat ever to run unopposed in a primary and then overwhelm the Republican nominee, Paul Eggers. In addition, the conservative Lloyd Bentsen won easily over the liberal Ralph Yarborough and then beat Congressman George Bush by warning labor and minorities that the senatorial duo of Bush and John Tower would support policies that would hurt their own interests.

In 1972, Texas voters turned against many longtime officeholders in the wake of another state government scandal—the Sharpstown Bank Scandal. Cartoonists did for the bank scandal what television did for the war as they heightened people's dissatisfaction with politicians. Matters were made worse when Gus Mutscher, speaker of the House, appointed his friends to investigate the charges and they found no wrongdoing among the accused. Cartoonists, led by Bob Taylor of the *Dallas Times Herald*, urged reform in the legislature. The result was seventy-two new members in the House and fifteen in the Senate. Governor Smith and Ben Barnes, the lieutenant governor and presumed heir to the governor's seat, were badly tainted by the scandal and were defeated for public office by millionaire businessman Dolph Briscoe.

Governor Briscoe brought a conservative philosophy to state government. He strongly supported increased spending for highway improvements and backed sound financing of state services. Through the 1970s successive governors Smith and Briscoe promised not to raise taxes and to increase revenues through economic growth. Texas remained a low-tax state, consistently ranking in the bottom ten nationally in taxes throughout those years.

Texas' population grew rapidly in the 1970s, with the attraction of the sunbelt to outside industries. The state moved past Ohio and Illinois and became the fourth most populous state in the country. As the state's population grew and changed, the voters abandoned their century-long tradition of electing Democratic governors. In 1978 an off-shore drilling contractor named Bill Clements startled Texas voters by spending $7 million of his own money to defeat former Texas attorney general John Hill by a narrow margin. With John Tower in the Senate, Texas was now beginning to be seen as a two-party state.

The 1970s marked numerous changes in the cartooning world as well. Bill McClanahan and Herc Ficklen both retired in this decade, first McClanahan, in 1972. In one of his last cartoons, McClanahan had Lefty Q Liberal, a cretin in beret and tennis shoes, delivering a swift kick to the likeness of McClanahan with Old Bill delivering the observation "He even kicks left footed." Ficklen hung up his pens in 1976, after his last cartoon appeared on December 31. He resumed the landscape painting he had abandoned as a teenager; he died in 1980. Despite the retirement of these two greats, the *Dallas Morning News* continued their tradition of editorial cartoons by bringing on Bill DeOre, *News* Sunday supplement art director, as the full-time editorial cartoonist.

But just as Texas lost two great masters, three more entered the scene in the 1970s and began to have a major impact in cartooning in the next decade. Ben Sargent joined the *Austin American-Statesman*; Jim Morin was hired by the *Beaumont Enterprise*; and Etta Hulme walked into a job at the *Fort Worth Star-Telegram*.

Ben Sargent, a native Texan from a newspaper family, went to junior college in Amarillo, then on to the University of Texas, where he got a degree in journalism in 1970 before joining the *American-Statesman* as a reporter in 1971. In addition to being a reporter, he also drew an occasional illustration before he asked the editor if he could draw an editorial cartoon. It was only a short time before he put down his reporter's notebook and picked up his triple-O brush and .35 millimeter technical pen full time.

Jim Morin was born in the politically charged area of Washington, D.C., and began drawing cartoons at the age of seven. The social and political upheavals during the sixties prompted an intense interest in current events. After graduating from Syracuse University in 1976, Morin began his editorial cartooning at the *Beaumont Enterprise*. He was there only a year before he moved to the *Richmond Times-Dispatch* and then to the *Miami Herald*, where he became a Pulitzer Prize finalist in 1979.

Etta Hulme, one of the first female editorial cartoonists in the country, found a home at the *Fort Worth Star-Telegram* in 1972. At that time Harold Maples's cartoons appeared only in the morning paper while a syndicated cartoonist from Buffalo, New York, was being carried for the afternoon paper. Apparently the "warm" Fort Worth was seeing too many "snow" cartoons and decided to find another cartoonist for the afternoon. In walked Ms. Hulme, who had done some cartooning for the *Texas Observer* and was in the area looking for a job. There was only one office for the cartoonists, so she ended up working at home. However, she was immediately well received by her colleagues and the city, despite once being defended by a misguided editor as a "harmless housewife."

"Disregard of the Law"
Bill McClanahan
January 22, 1970
Dallas Morning News

The 1960s demonstrations for civil rights and against the war in Vietnam created a schism in society. Frustrations with racism and the terrible conditions in the ghettos led to violent uprisings in Watts, Newark, Detroit, and other urban areas. Many conservatives saw the upheavals as an example of a permissive society that encouraged the breakdown of law and order. This cartoon suggests that reform and confrontations over issues of peace and justice led to the mindset that produced riots.

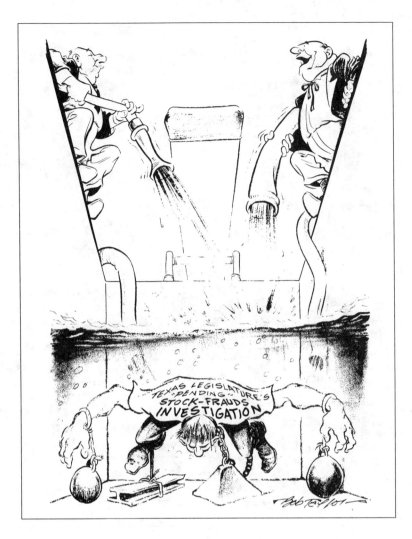

"Stock Fraud Investigation"
Bob Taylor
March 27, 1971
Dallas Times Herald

A bill sailed through the legislature in 1969 to exempt state banks from the regulations of the Federal Deposit Insurance Corporation. The bill was the product of Frank Sharp, who controlled the National Bankers Life Insurance Company and the Sharpstown State Bank. Legislators, Gov. Preston Smith, and House Speaker Gus Mutscher all had purchased stock in the insurance company, some with unsecured loans from the bank. After the bill passed, the stock was sold at above the market price. Sharp arranged the sale. Smith vetoed the banking bill after he sold his stock, saying that he had not originally realized the bill's significance. National Bankers Life went bankrupt. Mutscher, later convicted on charges of conspiracy and bribery, appointed a hand-selected group of legislators in the spring of 1971 to investigate charges of stock fraud. As this cartoon implies, the legislative committee attempted to bury the investigation. A coalition of conservative Republicans and liberal Democrats in the House refused to let the investigation die. This group became known as the "Dirty Thirty."

"—GET GOING, YOU HAVEN'T GOT ALL DAY"

"State Legislature Reapportionment"
Herc Ficklen
September, 1971
Dallas Morning News

The U.S. Supreme Court began to rule in the 1970s that states had to apportion their legislatures fairly by equalizing representation based on population. The Texas Legislature had to redraw its boundaries in 1971 based on the 1970 census. This redistricting occurred at the same time the "Dirty Thirty" were challenging Speaker Gus Mutscher's tactics. Consequently, the speaker picked a committee that would redraw his opponents' districts in a way that re-election would be difficult. The new House legislative map was a mishmash of lines that made no apparent sense. The district court struck down the legislative plan in January, 1972.

THE CONNALLY CAPER —

"The Connally Caper"
Herc Ficklen
March 11, 1973
Dallas Morning News

John Connally was a strong, conservative Democratic governor. His political strength held back the development of the Republican party in the state for at least a decade. Connally began to split with the Democratic party over Pres. Lyndon Johnson's civil rights legislation, but despite their differences the governor remained loyal to his friend, the president, throughout the sixties. Pres. Richard M. Nixon appointed Connally as secretary of the treasury, and he headed the president's attempts to control inflation in 1971. Rumors developed in 1972 that the nomination of George McGovern would cause the former governor to switch parties. He did so in 1973 and was rumored to be a contender for the presidency. He challenged for the Republican nomination in 1980 but conceded defeat to Ronald Reagan before the Texas primary took place.

"Finishing Up"
Harold Maples
May 5, 1972
Fort Worth Star-Telegram

The Sharpstown scandals opened the way for new legislative and gubernatorial races in 1972. Preston Smith announced for re-election. Lt. Gov. Ben Barnes, a favorite of John Connally and Lyndon Johnson, was the frontrunner. Although he was not connected to Sharpstown, the scandal had tainted all public officials by association. Frances "Sissy" Farenthold, an original member of the "Dirty Thirty," announced as a reform candidate. Dolph Briscoe, a millionaire rancher and former legislator, had the backing of a sizable wing of the conservative Democratic party. The election was very close, as this cartoon implies, but to the surprise of many observers Smith ran a bad fourth and Barnes failed to make the runoff. Briscoe beat Farenthold by about 200,000 votes in the second primary and was elected governor the next November.

"The Big Thicket Controversy"
Herc Ficklen
July 6, 1973
Dallas Morning News

As early as 1927, efforts were made to save and preserve the Big Thicket. The Little Thicket Nature Sanctuary, created by private funds, purchased some land in the 1950s, but by then conservationists argued that the federal government should take steps to protect the unique area. Sen. Ralph Yarborough introduced legislation in 1966 to create a national park preserving part of the East Texas Big Thicket area. The bill spent five years in committee and by the 1970s was a fierce source of political controversy. Plans varied from a 25,000-acre park of non-adjacent islands of vegetation to a 191,000-acre contiguous-area park. The controversy increased in 1973 with all key officials, including Governor Briscoe, involved. A compromise was struck in 1974 with an agreement to create a 84,500-acre Big Thicket National Preserve that consisted of island parks linked together by corridors. Pres. Gerald Ford signed the bill that year, and the land was purchased over the next six years.

"Eleventh Hour"
Harold Maples
January 4, 1975
Fort Worth Star-Telegram

Governor Briscoe won again in 1974, once more defeating Frances "Sissy" Farenthold. The governor promised that his administration would not raise taxes. Indeed, the governor brought about little in the way of change. He was a moderate conservative who made some good appointments and some accommodations with both Hispanics and labor unions. But overall, he was not considered by most observers as a particularly active or effective leader. In this cartoon Governor Briscoe is shown facing a second-term spate of urban problems that the legislature would have to consider.

"This baby has a wart...off with his head!"

—By BOB TAYLOR, Times Herald Staff Cartoonist

"This Baby Has a Wart . . ."
Bob Taylor
October 17, 1975
Dallas Times Herald

The Sharpstown scandal called forth a demand for reform. One concern centered on the writing of a constitution to replace the outmoded 1876 document. Most of the important newspapers and most state leaders endorsed such a move. The voters approved an amendment calling for a 1974 constitutional convention, composed of the legislature, to write a new document. The legislature appointed a special committee. The independent commission submitted a report to the legislature, which spent $5 million and several months, then refused to accept the commission's report or to submit the document to the people for ratification or rejection. The legislature revived the issue in 1975 by submitting to the public eight proposals which would have revised the 1876 constitution. The governor, who had exercised no leadership during the constitutional convention, opposed some revisions. The public, weary of the controversy, defeated the proposals by a three-to-one vote.

'Hi! Uh, I'm kinda new in the neighborhood and, well, do, uh, 'you-all' think I could borrow a cup of natural gas?...'

"Borrow a Cup of Natural Gas"
Jim Morin
1977
Beaumont Enterprise

The price per barrel of Texas crude oil stayed around four dollars until the major oil-producing countries formed the Organization of Petroleum Exporting Countries (OPEC). The 1974 Arab embargo on oil imports to the United States and other supporters of Israel ended a twenty-five-year state of stability in oil prices and caused the cost of petroleum products to soar. The Northeast was particularly hard-hit. In this cartoon, Texas' neighbors to the north are encouraging natural gas production and price controls to aid in overcoming spiraling costs. The collapse of the market in the mid-1980s sent the Texas economy downward and likewise lessened the demand that some national planning for the use of natural gas be implemented.

BIG TEX

"Big Tex"
Harold Maples
July 6, 1977
Fort Worth Star-Telegram

The Texas population grew rapidly in the 1970s with the attraction of the sunbelt to outside industries and the influx of immigration from Mexico. The oil boom served as a magnet, too, in that decade, as workers left the economic stagnation of the North for jobs in Texas. The census counted 11,198,655 Texans in 1970, moving the state population count past Ohio and Illinois and into fourth place nationally. The influx in the mid-seventies, as this cartoon celebrates, pushed Texas past Pennsylvania and ranked the state's population as number three, behind New York and California. Some experts predicted that Texas would soon replace New York as the second-largest state in population. But the downturn in the state economy limited migration into Texas, and its population of 16,986,510 persons in 1990 left it in the third spot.

"Boo to KKK"
Harold Maples
November 8, 1977
Fort Worth Star-Telegram

The Ku Klux Klan decided that on Halloween weekend, 1977, it would initiate its own border patrol in deep South Texas in an attempt to spot and report illegal aliens. The KKK reported that it sent out nearly two hundred men on patrol in response to what members saw as an ineffective Immigration and Naturalization Service. They claimed INS could never work well since its director was Hispanic.

Responding to this Halloween patrol was the group known as the Brown Berets, a Hispanic-based, quasi-militant group that pledged to keep the Klan from bothering Mexican-Americans. Apparently neither group confronted the other, but there were reports that a Spanish-language radio station aired a statement from a member of the Brown Berets warning against the Klan's activities and hinting at taking up arms against the KKK.

"Yarbrough the Martyr"
Bob Taylor
July 14, 1977
Dallas Times Herald

In 1976 Don Yarbrough was elected to serve on the Texas Supreme Court. The Houston attorney won despite the facts that he had already lost a civil fraud suit and that the State Bar of Texas had filed a disbarment suit against him two weeks before the election. He had fifteen additional civil suits pending against him. Yarbrough took his seat on the bench, but a Travis County grand jury indicted him on forgery and perjury charges.

The cartoon refers to action set by the legislature to have him removed from the bench. Reported to be a very religious man, Yarbrough attempted to weather the charges by claiming divine support and insisting that he was being persecuted by political enemies. The catsup bottle used to paint Yarbrough's tears indicates that most believed him to be a charlatan. Yarbrough never made it to the legislative trial as he resigned the day before it was scheduled to be held. Subsequently, Yarbrough was convicted of aggravated perjury and sentenced to serve two to five years in prison.

"Not Bad!"
Bill Saylor
November 10, 1978
Houston Post

In 1978 Gov. Dolph Briscoe announced for a third term. The affable
governor stressed his conservative philosophy and improvements of the
highway network. Nevertheless most observers expressed surprise when
the moderately liberal attorney general John Hill defeated the incumbent in the primary. The Republicans nominated William P. Clements,
Jr., a Dallas oilman who had supported Ronald Reagan in the party
fights of the 1970s. Hill ran a complacent campaign. Clements ran a
well-financed and well-organized one. The Republican defeated Hill
by a razor-thin margin, and Clements's election announced that Texas
was a two-party state. Republican senator John Tower also narrowly
retained his Senate seat. In this cartoon the Republicans celebrate
winning the gubernatorial election.

"Barking Dogs"
Charles Fincher
June, 1979
Brownsville Herald

The Ixtoc I offshore exploratory oil well blew out on June 3, 1979. The rig that had been drilling in the Bay of Campeche off the southern Mexican coast was destroyed in the blowout and began spewing oil. By August, the currents had carried the oil to South Texas beaches. Governor Bill Clements called the spill "a big t'do about nothing" and described those reporting the potential effects of the spill on Texas beaches as a "bunch of Chicken Littles." Mexican President Lopez Portillo called the reports of the spill and effects on Texas beaches "distorted reporting by the barking dogs of the press" and "internationally managed news distortion." After massive clean-up efforts, the beaches were freed of the sludge and not permanently damaged. South Padre Island suffered millions of dollars in losses to its tourist industry because of the spill.

"The Killer Bees"
Ben Sargent
1979
Unpublished

There was an attempt in 1979 to separate the presidential and state primary elections in Texas. Such a move would have allowed conservatives to vote in the Republican presidential primary for John Connally and then to vote later for conservative Democrats. Separate primaries, then, would not have forced conservatives to choose between parties. To block this move, a group of twelve liberal and moderate senators left the floor, preventing a quorum. Lt. Gov. William Hobby nicknamed this group the "Killer Bees." The "Killer Bees" eluded the Texas Rangers, who were sent to bring the missing legislators back to the capitol, and their absence killed the bill. The antics of the "Killer Bees" prevented separate primaries and probably protected the election of some moderate and liberal Democrats—as well as saving the state some money.

A Time of Change (1980–90)

In 1980, Ben Sargent produced what cartoon historian Richard West called the most "imaginative collection of cartoons ever produced." Sargent's book *Texas Statehouse Blues* gave new meaning to cartoon collection books as he attempted to explain Texas politics the old-fashioned way—as an artist, not a writer. Reminiscent of Jack Patton in his collection *Texas History Movies*, Sargent created a few characters who explained Texas politics as a comic book story based on previously published political cartoons.

But while Sargent was changing the look of cartooning, oil prices were changing the face of Texas. Oil and gas provided 28 percent of the state revenue in 1981 but only 12 percent in 1989; energy-related businesses had lost nearly 300,000 jobs by the end of the decade. Texas' strength of raising revenue through economic growth all but collapsed and the 1987–88 legislature passed a $5.7 billion tax bill, the largest of any in state history.

The recession also led to a decline in the once-strong banking industry. In 1989, approximately 1,700 Texas banks were on the ropes, with 59 banks closing in 1987 and another 113 in 1988. Bank failures in Texas exceeded those of the Great Depression, according to some economists.

Even the Texas farm economy ran into trouble. By the end of the decade the number of farms had declined to 156,000 from 180,000 at the beginning of 1980. Farmers were packing up and moving to the cities.

On the political side, with Governor Clements no longer an un-known, most observers thought he would have an easy time gaining a second four-year term in 1982. He was backed by the incumbency and a campaign war chest of over $13 million. He was opposed by state Attorney General Mark White who had won the nomination in a hard-fought primary against several opponents and was given little chance for victory.

But with Texas suffering with the rest of the nation from the worst economic recession since the Great Depression, anything could happen and did in the election. The poor economy attracted a large turn-out of Democrats, and even though Clements outspent White by a two-to-one margin, White's grass-roots appeal carried him to victory.

Governor White's administration was immediately hit with school-teachers' quarreling over educational reforms and prisons that were inadequately funded. Despite many successes the liberal governor accomplished, Texans questioned his leadership in a time of crisis, particularly over taxes. The result was that Clements announced for a rematch against Governor White in 1986.

The campaign rhetoric was vitriolic as White lost to Clements, with the Democrat receiving thrity-six thousand fewer votes than he had in 1982. It also was the most expensive campaign ever, as the candidates spent $25 million—that is, the most expensive until four years later when Ann Richards, the former state treasurer, challenged and beat Clayton Williams, a wealthy political unknown, to end the decade.

Gubernatorial elections were easy fodder for cartoonists, who were now able to draw about them only every four years rather than every two. As candidates changed, so did cartoonists. Though Etta Hulme continued with the *Fort Worth Star-Telegram*, Bill DeOre with the *Dallas Morning News*, and C. P. Houston with the *Houston Chronicle*, there were new cartoonists appearing on the scene in papers all over Texas. Mike Shelton and J. D. Crowe complemented Etta Hulme's work at the *Star-Telegram*; John Branch and John Darkow produced excellent work for the *San Antonio Express-News* and the *San Antonio Light*, respectively; Jimmy Margulies became an unsung treasure for the *Houston Post*; Bob Taylor continued his assassin's pen at the *Dallas Times Herald* until 1989 when he retired and traded his pen for golf clubs; Scott Willis and Dan Foote took over at the *Times Herald* and produced strong cartoons that created a healthy competition with DeOre at the *Dallas Morning News*; Charles Fincher started a syndicated political strip in which Thadeus and Weez, a scruffy lawyer and a short fat weasel, ridiculed Texas politics. Even smaller papers recognized the importance of an editorial cartoonist: Erkki Alanen cartooned for the *El Paso Times* and Mike Jenkins joined the *Beaumont Enterprise* from 1981 to 1984.

But while new cartoonists were appearing all over the state, the 1980s saw the death of three great cartoonists, Herc Ficklen, Harold Maples, and Bill McClanahan, all of whom had been drawing cartoons for the better part of a century. They had informed Texans with their wit and wisdom and pen and had drawn incisively about the times and affairs of the Lone Star State, the United States, and the world. Newspaper readers expressed great sadness and regret at their passing, for they were all nationally recognized as cartoonists of stature. In addition to being craftsmen at the drawing board with a gift for spotting and revealing the ridiculous in politics and sport, they were also gentle, agreeable men, good-humored and quick to the laugh. With John Knott, they were considered the fathers of editorial cartooning in Texas, and their work can be seen influencing the future of Texas cartoonists.

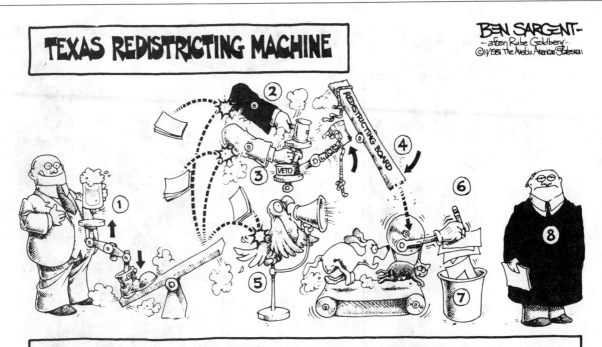

"Texas Redistricting Machine"
Ben Sargent
November, 1981
Austin American-Statesman

The Texas Legislature was required in 1981 to reapportion its legislative districts to conform to the 1980 census. A major struggle ensued, with the legislature wishing to protect incumbents, with minorities guaranteed that changes in the districts could not dilute the national Voting Rights Act, with liberals and Republicans wishing for more representative legislative districts, and with the Senate and the House responsible for reapportioning their own districts. Consequently the redistricting bills failed to satisfy any group. The Republican governor, Bill Clements, vetoed the Senate bill on the grounds that it discriminated against Republicans and minorities. He signed the House bill, which minorities then took to the courts; the Texas Supreme Court declared it unconstitutional. The Legislative Redistricting Board, composed of five Democrats, redrew the boundaries. The federal courts tossed out those plans and redrew some of the boundaries in 1982 to make them more racially and ethnically representative. As this cartoon shows, the process had a surreal, Rube Goldberg–like feel to it.

" ... GUESS WHO'S COMING TO DINNER?.."

By SCOTT WILLIS, Times Herald Editorial Cartoonist

"Guess Who's Coming to Dinner?"
Scott Willis
October 28, 1982
Dallas Times Herald

The 1978 gubernatorial election had marked two political firsts for Texas. The newly elected governor would now serve a four-year term, and the victor in that election, William P. Clements, Jr., a Dallas oilman with close ties to Ronald Reagan, was the first Republican governor of Texas in the twentieth century. The decade of the eighties thus began with a Republican in the Texas statehouse.

The Democrats nominated the state attorney general, Mark White, Jr., to lead a unified party challenge in 1982 against the Republican incumbent. Both White and Clements courted minority voters, who had registered in large numbers throughout the 1970s. All pundits noted, as this cartoon implies, that any candidate needed the critical minority vote in the state in order to win the election. In an upset victory, White won the race, garnering an astonishing 54 percent of the popular vote.

"Boot Hill"
Mike Shelton
June 2, 1983
Fort Worth Star-Telegram

The 68th session of the Texas Legislature, which concluded on May 30, 1983, achieved notoriety primarily for what it did not do. Gov. Mark White's call for higher pay for public school teachers came to nothing. A water conservation plan was defeated during the last few days of the session. Proposals for repealing the state's blue laws and appropriationg funds for highway upkeep died in committee. Calls for raising the drinking age and prohibiting open beverage containers in motor vehicles also were ignored. Most of the obstructionism took place in the House of Representatives. The House's Calendar Committee prevented so many Senate bills from appearing on the daily agenda that Senate aides began wearing buttons reading: "Will Rogers never met the Calendar Committtee." The *Fort Worth Star-Telegram*, in which this cartoon appeared, commented that the legislative session did not, as was customary, race across the finish line but rather "lurched to a stop like a car that has run out of gas."

"State Board of Education"
Mike Jenkins
February 4, 1984
Beaumont Enterprise

For the past seventy-odd years, controversies over the teaching of evolution in the public schools have surfaced intermittently. The State Board of Education, first created with the Gilmer-Aiken Act and then modified in the 1984 school reforms, has the responsibility of approving texts for adoption. The books are approved after public hearings, which have always been heated. As population has increased, so has controversy over content—for the sheer size of Texas has prompted publishers to tailor their books to the state's market. Opponents of teaching evolution argue that textbooks in Texas public schools should describe an alternative called "creation science" or present a biblical rebuttal to the theory of evolution. Proponents of evolution maintain that such alternate ideas are not only incorrect but also frustrate learning. As this cartoon shows, the State Board of Education has wanted most for the controversy simply to disappear. Recently the Texas Education Agency has adopted books with standard scientific interpretations, but it is unlikely that the controversy has ended.

JOSHUA AT THE WALLS OF JERICHO HIGH

"Joshua at the Walls of Jericho High"
Bob Taylor
October 18, 1984
Dallas Times Herald

Gov. Mark White appointed a select committee headed by Dallas businessman H. Ross Perot, a national folk hero who would later run for president, to report on the status of public schools. The legislature followed the committee's recommendation and adopted House Bill 72. The bill raised the mark for passing to 70, mandated special tutoring for students, created a master teacher classification, raised salaries, and limited class size, among other changes in administration and testing procedures. The more controversial section of the new law was "no pass–no play," which prohibited those who score below 70 in any subject from participating in extracurricular activities during the next six-week grade period. Here, Ross Perot is depicted as "Joshua" bringing down the walls that protected the hallowed ground of football. Criticism mounted against HB 72. Indeed, some observers ascribe much of the defeat of Governor White in 1986 to the defection of public school teachers and rural anger with "no pass–no play." Nevertheless, the reforms remained in place.

"Windfall Profits Tax"
J. D. Crowe
March, 1986
Fort Worth Star-Telegram

The 1974 Arab embargo on oil to the United States and other supporters of Israel destabilized oil prices and led to a roller coaster ride that
saw oil peak at forty dollars a barrel in 1980 and collapse to ten dollars
in 1986. During the period of price volatility, Pres. Jimmy Carter's
administration passed a windfall profit tax on oil. In 1986 President
Reagan proposed that the tax be repealed to stimulate new drilling.
Drilling did not increase, however. The price of oil rose and stabilized
at around twenty dollars per barrel, but that figure would not be high
enough to encourage much wildcatting. Indeed, Texas crude production peaked in 1972. Even though wells have pumped at full capacity
since then, production has dropped. Alaska replaced Texas in 1988 as
the leading producer of crude in the United States. The country
imports a higher percentage of oil now than before the 1974 boycott,
and most economists agree that never again will oil, a nonrenewable
resource, dominate the Texas economy.

Texas celebrated its 150th birthday in 1986.

"Sesquicentennial"
Jimmy Margulies
March, 1986
Houston Post

The Rio Grande has historically been a false border with populations on either side relying on mutually dependent economies. The pull and push of immigration, moreover, has been a matter of depressed economic areas sending their dispossessed into lands of economic opportunity. The combination of the poverty of Mexico and the prosperity of Texas in the 1970s and early 1980s sent a flood of immigrants across an unenforceable boundary. The result has been similar to the Texas Revolution in reverse, as anxious immigrants have moved into Texas searching for opportunities. The federal government passed an Immigration Reform and Control Act in 1986. Most commentators question the effectiveness of the act in ending the flow of undocumented workers. The U.S. Census of 1990 reported that the number of Texans of Hispanic descent was roughly 25 percent of the state's population. Many observers consider that figure an undercount because of the difficulty of recording urban ethnic and racial minorities in general and the counting of illegal aliens in particular.

"On His Way"
John Darkow
September 23, 1986
San Antonio Light

San Antonio gained national recognition when Henry Cisneros became the first Hispanic mayor of a major U.S. city in May of 1981. He was known for staying close to his roots. He and his wife raised their family in the neighborhood he grew up in, which was in the area of town with the lowest per capita income. As mayor, he continued to drive the family car—a Volkswagen—and he gave speeches in both Spanish and English. During his first term, Cisneros "rolled up his sleeves" and went to work—occasionally collecting garbage and riding in squad cars on patrol.

His charm, his youth, and his ethnicity led the media, among others, to speculate about higher aspirations he might have. While he never publicly announced that he was pursuing an office beyond mayor, he also never denied the possibility of further career goals. When his final term as mayor was over in May of 1989, Cisneros went into private business, but in 1993 he would become secretary of Housing and Urban Development under Pres. Bill Clinton.

"THIRTY-TWO DEGREES! DO YOU REALIZE WHAT THIS MEANS? THE TEXAS LEGISLATURE MUST BE CONSIDERING AN INCOME TAX."

"Thirty-Two Degrees"
Etta Hulme
1988
Fort Worth Star-Telegram

One constant political issue in Texas has been from whom and how taxes should be collected. Texas' tax structure has been a crazy-quilt of compromise, with most revenue since 1962 derived from a sales tax. The easiest way to raise taxes has been to add to the sales tax and to include goods originally exempted. The collapse of oil prices eliminated 25 percent of the state's revenue and sent the legislature scurrying for new money. The state Constitution mandated a balanced budget, and the legislature raised taxes three times between 1984 and 1987. The 1987 sales tax increase came at the same time that state sales taxes ceased to be deductible from federal income taxes. The legislature thus authorized a Select Committee on Tax Equity, which concluded in 1988 that a restructuring of state taxes was essential for fairness and economic growth. The legislature refused to respond. Texas had no income tax as of 1993 but has been under chronic pressure to consider options for tax monies.

"Thadeus and Weez"
Charles Fincher
January 29, 1988
Syndicated Strip

The issue of prison reform popped up again in 1980 when U.S. District Judge Wayne Justice ordered the state to correct problems in overcrowding, health and safety standards, and prison brutality. Governor Clements vetoed a bill in 1981 which would have built more prisons. When the court ruled in Clements's second term that the prisons could not exceed 95 percent capacity, the governor relied on early release and the sale of $500 million in bonds to fund new prisons. The bonds did not sell as rapidly as hoped. This cartoon charges the governor with avoiding the issue of financing additional prison beds. The issue will likely remain a source of consternation for legislatures for years to come.

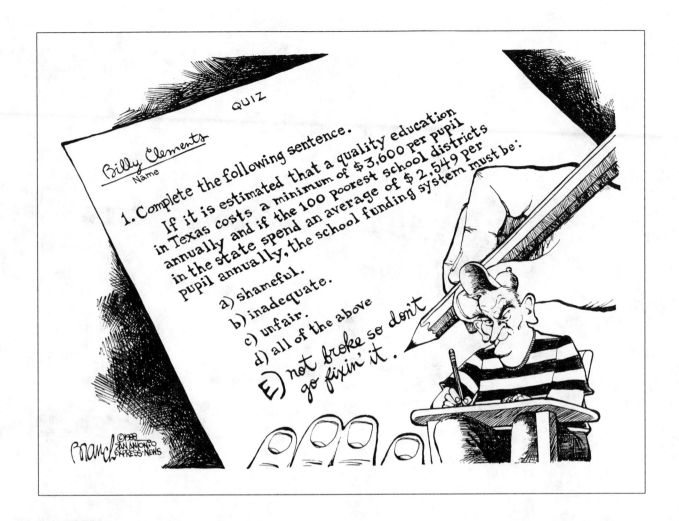

"Not Broke So Don't Go Fixin' It"
John Branch
1988
San Antonio Express-News

The issue of equality in financing of the public schools went to the courts in 1968. The complicated system of financing the public schools provided state payments of more than $5 billion to the $9 billion public school system. The subsequent disparities in local property taxes allowed the one hundred wealthiest districts to spend some $7,200 per pupil compared with less than $3,000 in the poorest one hundred districts. State District Judge Harley Clark ruled that the state system of financing public schools was unconstitutional because of the inequality in spending per pupil. Governor Clements wanted a constitutional amendment that would legitimize the previous method of financing public schools. Unable to convince the legislature to propose such an amendment, the governor appointed a fifteen-member board to evaluate the problem.

BANK & LOAN

FINANCIAL INSTITUTION REGULATORS

©89 Fincher

REVENGE OF THE NERDS—THE TEXAS SEQUEL

2-25-89

"Revenge of the Nerds"
Charles Fincher
February 25, 1989
Austin American-Statesman

In December, 1977, Texas had 328 savings and loan associations. These organizations and banking institutions took advantage of the boom years of oil and real estate growth and changes in federal regulations to enjoy a period of unparalleled prosperity and expansion. With the collapse of the Texas economy and the nationwide savings and loan debacle, Texas financial institutions went bankrupt with depressing regularity. In 1991 there existed only 131 savings and loans institutions in the state—and 51 of those were in federal conservatorship. Moreover, the 10 largest state bank corporations as of 1986 had by 1990 become the property of out-of-state banks. No one knows what the collapse of these institutions will eventually cost taxpayers. The issue, however, persists.

"Defense Cuts"
Dan Foote
April 27, 1989
Dallas Times Herald

It had been argued that the Texas economy once rested on the three-legged stool of agriculture, defense, and oil. The collapse of the oil industry in the mid-1980s and the problems of farmers throughout the decade heightened Texas' awareness of the importance of defense. Secretary of Defense Dick Cheney recommended in 1989 that several military bases, including Bergstrom Air Force Base in Austin and Carswell Air Force Base in Fort Worth, be shut down. This cartoon responds to Cheney's argument that the defense cuts would have little economic impact. The issue of the "peace dividend" has intensified since the collapse of the Soviet Union. The Bergstrom base was returned by the federal government to Austin, for example, and will probably become an airport. Recent predictions, however, list first Missouri and then Texas as the states that will suffer most dramatically from the defense cuts. It looks unlikely that the state will ever again rely on defense.

"Damned Pesticides"
Jay Carr
April 7, 1989
Pine Log

The 1982 gubernatorial campaign confounded political prognosticators when Democratic candidates buried previous feuds and created an "umbrella" campaign that elected Mark White, Jr., as governor, Bill Hobby as lieutenant governor, Ann Richards as state treasurer, Jim Mattox as attorney general, Garry Mauro as land commissioner, and Jim Hightower as agriculture commissioner. Hightower, a former editor of the progressive *Texas Observer*, earned both national notoriety and the hostility of conservatives in the Farm Bureau and the agribusiness industries over his outspoken liberal support of farm workers and regulation of pesticides. After former governor Bill Clements defeated White for re-election in 1986, there was a move by conservatives to limit Hightower's power by making his office appointive rather than elective. A compromise was struck which removed much of the commissioner's control over the regulation of pesticides. Hightower was defeated by Republican Rick Perry in 1990, and the attempt to further restrict the office of agriculture commissioner has faded as an issue.

"The 1st Pilgrim"
Brad McMillan
July 24, 1989
City Life

Lonnie "Bo" Pilgrim appeared in the Texas Senate in July, 1989, passing out ten thousand–dollar checks to selected senators just before a vote on a workers' compensation law that the East Texas chicken magnate opposed. It was reported by the press that Pilgrim had previously given money to then attorney general Jim Mattox at a time when his office was investigating the entrepreneur's Pilgrim's Pride corporation. Although Pilgrim denied intent to influence, his actions led to a new call for an ethics reform bill. Governor Clements refused to include such a bill on the agenda for the special session called in 1989.

"Delicate Balance"
Erkki Alanen
El Paso Times
September 30, 1989

School reforms that included bureaucratic red tape and promised but unrealized teachers' raises left teachers carrying a heavy burden when school started in 1989. Attempts to get relief for them had repeatedly come to nothing; this cartoon by Erkki Alanen portrays the state of affairs after yet one more go-round in fine-tuning the reforms and the funding.

"A Recap of the 1990 Governor's Race"
Chris Britt
1990
Houston Post

The 1990 gubernatorial campaign followed a time-honored Texas tradition: it was bitter and it was personal. One of the most expensive races in Texas history, it included actively contested primaries for both parties, won by political newcomer Clayton Williams for the Republicans and former state treasurer Ann Richards for the Democrats. In a campaign marked by personal attacks that seemed excessive even by Texas' standards, Williams fell from a fifteen-point lead in the polls one month before the election to lose the race.

"A Recap of the 1990 Governor's Race"
Chris Britt
1990
Houston Post

The 1990 gubernatorial campaign followed a time-honored Texas tradition: it was bitter and it was personal. One of the most expensive races in Texas history, it included actively contested primaries for both parties, won by political newcomer Clayton Williams for the Republicans and former state treasurer Ann Richards for the Democrats. In a campaign marked by personal attacks that seemed excessive even by Texas' standards, Williams fell from a fifteen-point lead in the polls one month before the election to lose the race.

The Cartoonists

Erkki Alanen (1942–)

Born in Helsinki, Finland. Studied architecture in Finland. In 1972, immigrated to the United States. Began designing buildings in Ohio but decided to become a cartoonist and graphic designer. Moved to San Francisco and later to Key West, Florida, looking for the right environment—which he finally found in 1987 with the *El Paso Times*. His cartoons have been reproduced in about twenty European publications.

Talbot O. Bateman (1878–1938)

Born in Jefferson, Texas. Humorist and practical joker, he found himself sometimes the butt of his own pranks and symbolized this situation by adopting a goat as his mascot. The Bateman Goat appeared in most of his cartoons, dispensing marginal commentary. After college Bateman started cartooning on the *Fort Worth Evening Mail*, an afternoon Democratic paper. When a morning Republican paper began, an arrangement was made for Bateman to draw cartoons for both. He also worked for the *Fort Worth Register*, *Fort Worth Record*, *Dallas Journal*, *San Antonio Express*, and *Dallas News*.

Bert Blessington (1870–1939)

Born in Des Moines. One of the South's best-known newspaper artists at the turn of the century. Drew a front-page cartoon for the *Houston Post* for three decades, as well as inside drawings on politics, sports, and miscellany. He was a wiry red-haired fellow who handled a camera as well as he did a pencil. Known for his unfailing good humor and an ability to accept unpleasant developments with philosophic calm. Adults knew him through his published cartoons, but for many years children knew him through weekly school visits, where Blessington illustrated poems read by teachers. He left the *Post* in 1932 to enter commercial art.

John Grimes Branch (1953–)

Born in Durham, North Carolina. Raised in Chapel Hill. Attended University of North Carolina 1971–76 and graduated with a degree in studio art. Editorial cartoonist for *Daily Tar Heel* (campus newspaper) 1975–76, editorial cartoonist for the *Chapel Hill Newspaper* 1976–80, editorial cartoonist for *San Antonio Express* since 1981.

Chris Britt (1959–)

Born in Phoenix, Arizona. Began cartooning for the *Arizona Business Gazette* in 1989 before joining the *Sacramento Union* in 1990, and then the *Houston Post* from 1990–91. In 1991 he joined the *Morning News Tribune* in Tacoma, Washington. He is syndicated with the Coply News Service, and his work has been seen on CNN. He was the winner of the Excellent Achievement award in the John Fischetti cartoon competition in 1990 and won Best Editorial Cartoon from the Katie Award Press Club of Dallas, Planned Parenthood, and American Cancer Society.

Jay Ramsey Carr (1967–)

Editorial cartoonist, 1985–90, for the *Pine Log*, student newspaper of Stephen F. Austin State University at Nacogdoches, Texas. National winner, 1990 Society of Professional Journalists Mark of Excellence Award for collegiate editorial cartooning. Finalist, 1989 Scripps Howard Foundation National Journalism Awards. Currently staff artist for the *Austin Amerian-Statesman*.

Hal Coffman (1883–1958)

Born in Los Angeles. He secured his first cartooning job in 1898 with the *San Francisco Post*, where he worked for three dollars a week. Coffman was one of the first to work on a comic cartoon book. He was on the staff of Hearst's *New York Journal and American*. In 1906 he went to the *Philadelphia Inquirer*, where he gained fame for drawing accurate, realistic vistas from memory. He joined the *Fort Worth Star-Telegram* in 1939; he drew there for the next sixteen years in a style that mixed incisiveness with philosophical humor on a daily basis. He twice won medals from the Freedom Foundation for cartoons contributing to the American way of life.

J. D. Crowe (1959–)

Born in Kentucky. Graduate of Eastern Kentucky University with a B.F.A. in Design. Editorial cartoonist for the *Fort Worth Star-Telegram* 1983-87. Produced three to five editorial cartoons a week and a weekly cartoon panel called *Crowe's Feats*. Editorial cartoonist for the *San Diego Tribune* 1987–92. Designer, author, and artist of *Daze of Glory: Images of Fact and Fantasy Inspired by the Gulf War*; illustrated Jerry Flemmons's *Plowboys, Cowboys, and Slanted Pigs*. Winner of numerous awards, including California Newspaper Publishers Association, 1987; Society of Professional Journalists, 1989; and a finalist in the National John Fischetti editorial cartoon competition, 1989.

Tom Darcy (1932–)

Born in Brooklyn, New York. Received his art education at the School of Visual Arts in New York. Began his editorial cartooning in 1959 at *Newsday* and then developed his craft at the *Houston Post* from 1964 to 1966 and later at the *Philadelphia Bulletin*. In 1968, Bill Moyers, then publisher of *Newsday*, brought Darcy back to Long Island as editorial cartoonist. In 1970 he was awarded the Pulitzer Prize. He is also the recipient of numerous other awards, including the Meeman Conservation Award, National Headliners Award, Society of Silurian's Award, New York Page One Award, Margaret Sanger Award, RFK Citation for Excellence Award, and the National Achievement Award for Excellence in the Fischetti cartoon competition.

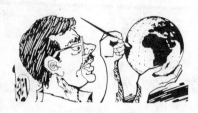

John Darkow (1956–)

Born in Madison, Wisconsin. Grew up in Columbia, Missouri. He attended the University of Missouri, where he drew cartoons for the college newspaper. For ten years, beginning in 1982, he was the political cartoonist for the *San Antonio Light*.

William (Bill) DeOre (1947–)

Born in Youngstown, Ohio. Received bachelor's degree in advertising art and design in 1970 from Texas Tech University, Lubbock. Began working for the *Dallas Morning News* in 1970 in the advertising department. At the *News* he developed friendships with cartoon masters Bill McClanahan and Herc Ficklen. In 1974 he began publishing one sports cartoon a week and in 1976 became a fulltime cartoonist. He is syndicated by the Universal Press Syndicate and was the winner of the John Fischetti Award for Outstanding Editorial Cartoon in 1983.

Lambert Der (1953–)

Born in Durham, North Carolina. Received a bachelor's degree in zoology (1975) and a master's in product design (1978) from North Carolina State University. Was a contributing cartoonist to the *Technician* (NCSU newspaper) and the *Raleigh Times* (1978–89) as well as a free-lance editorial cartoonist for the *Greensboro News and Record* (1980–85). He was the editorial cartoonist for the *Greenville News* (1985–91) before joining the *Houston Post* in 1991. He won first prize in the John Fischetti editorial cartoon competition in 1989. Was also the recipient of the Katie Award in 1992 from the Press Club of Dallas as well as first place for editorial cartoons from the Houston Press Club in 1991.

M. A. Dunning (?)

Born in Mississippi and reared in San Antonio. Received his training at the Cleveland Art Institute. He joined the *Austin American-Statesman* in 1938 after serving as a cartoonist for the *Houston Post*, the *San Diego Tribune*, and the *Atlanta Constitution*. He was also a member of Walt Disney's staff, where he participated in the making of *The Three Little Pigs*, a 1933 Oscar-winning film.

Bob Eckhardt (1913–)

Born in Austin, Texas. First began drawing during the First World War, where he used the sidewalk as his sketchpad. Drew cartoons under the name Jack O'Diamonds for the *Texas Spectator* from 1946 to 1949. Served in the Texas House of Representatives from 1958 to 1966. The next fourteen years he spent as a U.S. Congressman from Houston. He continues to draw political cartoons and is currently writing articles on the environment, energy, and politics while sitting in a treehouse from an ancient oak tree in his front yard. He is also working on a book entitled *Why Not Try the Constitution*.

Jack Howells (Herc) Ficklen (1911–80)

Nicknamed at an early age "Herc," short for "Hercules," because of the ease with which he destroyed sand castles. Herc grew up in Waco, Houston, and Dallas. Studied art at Southern Methodist University in Dallas before the depression forced him to abandon formal education. His first newspaper job was as a copy boy with the *Dallas Morning News*. He became interested in cartooning and began submitting sports and editorial cartoons. Began a regular sports cartoon in 1937. In 1946, after the war, he started doing editorial cartoons, alternating daily with John Knott and later Bill McClanahan. Retired from the *News*, with his last cartoon appearing December 31, 1976. In addition to his editorial cartoons, he also syndicated the popular cartoon series *Out of Orbit* in the 1950s, *Key Peek* in the 1960s, and *Avalon Features* in the 1960s and 1970s. Ficklen received numerous awards and honors during his career, including twelve Freedom Foundation Awards and five Katie Awards.

Charles Pugsley Fincher

At a very early age, Fincher says, he was tragically separated from his parents during a fishing expedition in the Okefenokee Swamp. Fortunately, he was found by Albert the Alligator, who with help from Pogo and Churchy la Femme raised him. Unsurprisingly, Fincher decided to be a cartoonist at the age of five. But knowing something about the financial perils of cartooning, the three surrogate parents insisted Fincher become a lawyer as well. Fed up with swamp mosquitoes, Fincher now lives on South Padre Island with lovely Laura, five dogs, and several determined cats. He lives in obscurity except for friends wanting a free place to stay on the beach.

Dan Foote (1960–)

Born in Madison, Ohio. Began his career at several small suburban newspapers in northeast Ohio. Began at the *Dallas Times Herald* in 1989 after a brief stint in New Jersey. He was the 1990 winner of the Katie, a Texas journalism award, for best editorial cartoon.

Etta Hulme (1923–)

Born in Summerville, Texas. Received a Bachelor of Fine Arts degree from the University of Texas in 1944. Her experience includes work in animation, comic-book illustration, and commercial art. Joined the *Fort Worth Star-Telegram* in 1972 as editorial cartoonist. Syndicated by Newspaper Enterprise Association. Received Best Editorial Cartoonist Award from the National Cartoonist Society in 1982.

Mike Jenkins (1956–)

Born in Evanston, Illinois, and raised in Richmond, Virginia. Graduated from the College of William and Mary with a bachelor's degree in government in 1980. With the *Beaumont Enterprise* from 1981 to 1984 and then with Journal Newspapers in the Washington, D.C., metro area since 1984. Also worked as a caricaturist at Astroworld Amusement Park in Houston, Six Flags over Georgia in Atlanta, and Kings Dominion in Doswell, Virginia.

SKETCH OF THE ARTIST by himself

John Knott (1878–1963)

Born in Austria. Moved to Chicago, then on to Texas in 1901 to do drafting work and Indian fighting. Joined *Dallas Morning News* in 1905, where he began doing editorial cartoons in 1911. Created Old Man Texas, a character who was to the state what Uncle Sam was to the nation. Stood for honesty in government, low taxes, and property ownership. His cartoons had a significant impact during World War I, and he encouraged the purchase of war bonds. Received honorable mention for a Pulitzer in 1936. His favorite cartoonists were J. N. "Ding" Darling, Rollin Kirby, and John T. McCutcheon. Continued with the *Dallas Morning News* until 1957, when he retired.

Harold Maples (1925–81)

Born in Petit, Texas, the son of two teachers who were also very good artists. Came out of the Navy in 1946 determined to do something with his artistic bent. Attended art school in Dallas and majored in art at McMurry College in Abilene. Sold free-lance cartoons until 1954, when the *Fort Worth Star-Telegram* began searching for a cartoonist to succeed the nationally famous Hal Coffman, who was approaching retirement. Loved the outdoors and once said that if he weren't a cartoonist he would be either a biologist for the forest service or a forest ranger. Produced more than seven thousand cartoons for the *Star-Telegram* over a twenty-seven-year period before he died. He also was an accomplished watercolor artist.

Jimmy Margulies (1951–)

Born in Brooklyn, New York. Holds a B.F.A. degree in graphic design from Carnegie-Mellon University in Pittsburgh. While attending college, began drawing editorial cartoons for the campus newspaper. Published work since the 1970s has garnered numerous awards from the Freedom Foundation, National Newspaper Association and the Maryland-DC-Delaware Press Association. In 1984 he joined the *Houston Post* as editorial cartoonist and won the Western Hemisphere Award and the Global Media Award from the Population Institute. In 1990, he became the first editorial cartoonist for the *Record*.

Ferman Martin (1899–1977)

Born in Lindale, in East Texas. Had studied art formally, but was largely self-tutored. Sold his first cartoon in 1925 for two dollars, after he answered a correspondence-school advertisement. Joined the *Houston Chronicle* in 1937 after pestering the managing editor for months with cartoons submitted by postcard. Worked until 1964 for the *Chronicle*, where he created "Mr. Houston" and "Mr. Texas" as symbolic characters. He won many awards, especially from veterans groups, and was once made chairman of the Cartoonists Council for the Disabled American Veterans.

William J. (Bill) McClanahan (1907–81)

Born in Greenville, Texas. Began his career as a sportswriter covering high-school football games for the *Dallas Morning News*. After his discharge from the service, he found his true vocation as a cartoonist. He returned to the sports staff in 1946 and divided his time between writing, editing, and drawing cartoons. First sports cartoon appeared on August 4, 1946. He is best remembered as the father of the Southwest Conference cartoon mascots, and he popularized the "Grid Gram," a visual box score of football games. In 1957, he joined Herc Ficklen as a fellow editorial cartoonist for the *News*, a position McClanahan held until retirement in 1972. He won numerous awards, including the Southwest Journalism Forum Award (1970), six Freedom Foundation Awards, the Congress of Freedom Liberty Award, and the 1972 Heila Temple Award. He died in 1981; three years later his wife, Eloise, donated many of his cartoons to the Dallas Public Library.

Brad McMillan (1946–)

Born in Jackson, Tennessee. He began his career in Memphis in the mid-seventies by selling drawings and watercolors to the public through galleries. He has contributed to numerous publications in the South, and in 1983 he became staff illustrator and editorial cartoonist for the *Memphis Business Journal*. He retains that position, even though he moved to Dallas, Texas, in 1986. He has done editorial cartoons and cartoon illustrations for the *Dallas Observer*, the *Dallas Downtown News*, *City Life*, the *Dallas Business Journal*, the *Dallas Weekly*, and the *Advocate*. His work has been reprinted in numerous publications across the country and has won the National Newspaper Association's Merit Award for best editorial cartoon. McMillan is currently drawing and producing video editorial cartoons for the Dallas PBS television station, KERA.

Jim Morin (1953–)

Born in Washington, D.C. He started drawing cartoons at the age of seven, taking as his initial influences the animated cartoons of Walt Disney, Jay Ward, Bob Clampett, and Hanna-Barbera. He began drawing editorial cartoons for the student newspaper, the *Daily Orange*, at Syracuse University. After graduating in 1976, he drew for the *Beaumont Enterprise and Journal*, followed by a year at the *Richmond Times-Dispatch* before he settled at the *Miami Herald* in 1978. He was a Pulitzer finalist in 1979 and 1990 and won both the Overseas Press Club Award and the Florida ACLU Media Award in 1989. His books outside the political area include *Famous Cars* (1982) and *Jim Morin's Field Guide to Birds* (1985).

Sam Nash (1906–)

Born at Richland, near Corsicana, Texas. Enjoyed drawing murals on his family's parlor wall at an early age. After completing chores on the family farm, he would work on a correspondence course in art. Graduate of the University of Texas and the Art Institute of Chicago. From 1922 to 1930, he and his father were in the sign-painting business, though cartooning was Sam's first love. In 1936 he began work on the *Tyler Courier-Times*, where he drew cartoons and operated engraving machinery. After service in World War II, he returned to Tyler and resumed his editorial cartoons for the *Courier-Times*. Created Old Man Tyler, a rotund, balding, and bespectacled character who appeared whenever Nash wanted to speak his mind.

William Kleevil Patrick (1873–1936)

Born in St. Louis, Missouri. Started newspaper work as a reporter on the *St. Louis Post-Dispatch*, writing and illustrating a weekly column called "Odd Observations." Briefly joined the staff of the *Houston Post* in 1896, where he worked with William Sydney Porter. Later, he worked as a chalk-plate artist for the *Dallas News* and the *Galveston News*. He was a member of the *Fort Worth Record* staff in 1910, then left to serve as cartoonist for the *New Orleans Picayune*. Returned to Fort Worth about 1920 as cartoonist for the *Fort Worth Star-Telegram*. In 1924 he joined the art department of the *San Antonio Express*, where he stayed for the next eleven years. He popularized a duck as his signature mascot.

THE LION IN HIS LAIR

Jack I. Patton (1900–62)

Born in Shreveport, Louisiana, he was five when he moved with his family to Dallas. Enrolled in the Academy of Fine Arts in Chicago. While at the school he received word that the *Dallas Journal*, the evening publication of the *Dallas News*, needed an assistant in the art department. He got the job in 1918, and by 1920 his editorial cartoons had won a place on Page 1 of the *Journal*. He was one of the few daily newspaper cartoonists to produce both an editorial cartoon and a comic strip. In the 1920s he initiated a comic strip *The Restless Age*, which in 1939 was syndicated under the title *Spence Easley*.

Clyde Peterson (1942–)

Born in Covington, Tennessee. It was in high school in Bartlett, Tennessee, that he refined his ambition for drawing in general to cartooning in particular. After drawing training aids and posters for the army, he took jobs writing advertising copy, running a laundry house, working in a lumberyard, and selling insurance. Then he decided to become a hobo and hitchhike around the country, carrying only a change of clothing and a sketch pad. Drew caricatures in bars and on street corners. On the advice of a cartoonist at the *Arkansas Gazette*, he went to art school in Houston. After school, he drew eight sample cartoons and left them for the editor of the *Houston Chronicle*, requesting information on how to become a cartoonist. Instead, the paper hired him as its editorial cartoonist on December 21, 1965. He has been the *Chronicle*'s cartoonist ever since. His cartoons appear under the pen name C. P. Houston. He is part of a team that writes and illustrates nationally distributed social studies material for secondary school students.

William Sydney Porter (1862–1910)

Born on a plantation near Greensboro, North Carolina. Moved to Austin in 1884. Worked as a draftsman for the land commissioner's office, where he drew maps for deeds. In 1891, Porter took a job at the First National Bank of Austin. In 1984 he founded a weekly newspaper called the *Rolling Stone*, in which he drew cartoons and wrote stories. The newspaper lasted only a year after he lost his bank-teller job because of shortages in the books. He left town and worked as an editorial cartoonist for the *Houston Post*. After eight months in Houston, he was indicted for embezzlement from the Austin bank. He fled to Honduras but became lonely for his family and returned to Austin to take care of his ailing wife while awaiting trial. It was during this period that he sold his first short story to a national publication (1897). He was found guilty and spent three and a half years in the penitentiary, where he perfected his literary craft. As he began to sell stories, he did not want to use his real name and finally settled on O. Henry as a pseudonym. After prison he moved to New York, where he published 381 stories over an eight-year period.

Dwane Powell (1944–)

Born in Lake Village, Arkansas; graduated from the University of Arkansas at Monticello with a degree in Agri-Business. Began as a reporter-cartoonist with the *Hot Springs Sentinel Record*. He was then an editorial cartoonist for the *Cincinnati Enquirer* and the *San Antonio Light* (1972–74). He joined the staff of the *Raleigh News and Observer* in 1975 and has received the National Headliners Award and Oversees Press Citation for Excellence. In 1979, Powell became a Distinguished Alumnus of the University of Arkansas at Monticello.

Ben Sargent (1948–)

Born in Amarillo, Texas, into a newspaper family. Learned the printing trade from age twelve and started working for the local daily as a proof runner at fourteen. Received a Bachelor of Journalism degree from the University of Texas in 1970. Started drawing editorial cartoons for the *Austin American-Statesman* in 1974 after working as a political reporter for the *Corpus Christi Caller-Times* and a newswire service. Winner of the 1982 Pulitzer Prize. Other accolades include Oustanding Communicator Award (1981), Texas Women's Political Caucus Media Award (1982), Mencken Award (1988), Outstanding Young Texas Exes (1989), and Common Cause of Texas Public Service Award in Journalism (1990). Author of *Texas Statehouse Blues* (1980) and *Big Brother Blues* (1984).

Wilford (Bill) Saylor (1914–)

Born in Comanche, Texas. Attended the Chicago Art Institute before receiving his Bachelor of Arts degree. He joined the *Houston Post* as political cartoonist in 1938 and worked there until World War II. After the war he earned a Bachelor of Arts degree from the University of Texas and a Master of Fine Arts from the University of Oklahoma. During those years he also worked on the short-lived, sassy *Texas Spectator* with Bob Eckhardt. He taught art at the University of Houston (1952–55) before he returned to the *Houston Post* as their editorial cartoonist. He created "Mr. Weatherby," a one-column cartoon feature regarding local events, which ran daily on the front page of the newspaper. He also did five political cartoons weekly until his retirement in 1979.

Mike Shelton (1951–)

Born in Houston. Grew up in San Jacinto County. After graduating from Coldspring High School, he enlisted in the Marine Corps, serving six years, including a tour in Vietnam. Shelton attended Sam Houston State University in Huntsville, Texas, where he studied art. He started his cartooning career with the Copley News Service Syndicate and later joined the *Fort Worth Star-Telegram* as a staff editorial cartoonist. After a year in Fort Worth, he moved west in 1983 to become editorial cartoonist for the *Orange County Register* in Santa Ana, California, his current position. His work is distributed nationally by King Features Syndicate.

Robert (Bryon) Taylor (1932–)

Born in Stockton, California. Raised and educated on the West Coast. Majored in education and minored in art and journalism at the University of California at Sacramento. Drew sports cartoons for the *Sacramento Union* while in college. Entered the Air Force after school and was stationed in San Antonio, where he served as academic instructor and art director for the base newspaper. While still in the Air Force, he sent out 250 copies of a tabloid called *Taylor Horntoot* in an effort to find work after uniformed service. The *Dallas Times Herald* made him its first editorial cartoonist in 1958, and he stayed there until he retired in 1989. He was winner of numerous awards, including the Headliners Award in 1986 and the prestigious Katie Award twelve different times. He is currently living in California and has lowered his golf handicap by four strokes.

Sidney Van Ulm (1893–1978)

Born in Boston, Massachussetts. Studied art at the New School of Design, where he also taught cartooning. Started cartooning on the *Boston Record* in 1914. His duties included sketching personalities, courtroom trials, theatrical stars, and sports figures. Came to Houston in 1921 as the staff artist on the *Houston Post*. In 1924, he began drawing primarily local cartoons for the *Houston Press*, which he did for the next forty-two years until the paper closed and forced him into retirement.

Scott Willis (1957–)

Born in Columbus, Ohio. Began cartooning as a journalism student at Ohio State University. During his senior year, he won the Sigma Delta Chi Mark of Excellence Award for college cartoonists in 1979. He began his professional career in 1980 with the *Cleveland Press*. He moved to Dallas, Texas, in 1982 to cartoon for the *Dallas Times Herald*, where he won the Katie Award in 1984. He joined the staff of the *San Jose Mercury News* in 1985 and won the Fischetti Award that same year. Was a finalist for the Fischetti Award in 1986 and 1988 and a finalist for the 1991 Mencken Award for a cartoon on freedom of speech.